Myanmar in Moments

Leo Lazarus

Myanmar in Moments

Myanmar in Moments
ISBN 978 1 76041 857 1
Copyright © Leo Lazarus 2020

First published 2020 by
Ginninderra Press
PO Box 3461 Port Adelaide 5015
www.ginninderrapress.com.au

Contents

1	Yangon	7
2	Yangon to Ngwesaung	13
3	Ngwesaung to Chaungtha	17
4	Chaungtha	23
5	Chaungtha	28
6	Chaungtha	31
7	Chaungtha to Pathein, Ngathaingehaun and Gwa	35
8	Gwa to Linn Thar	38
9	Linn Thar	41
10	Linn Thar and Thandwe	46
11	Linn Thar to Taungup	49
12	Taungup to Sittwe	53
13	Sittwe to Mrauk-U	58
14	Mrauk-U	63
15	Mrauk-U	67
16	Mrauk-U	72
17	Mrauk-U to Magway	76
18	Magway to Nyaung-U	79
19	Nyaung-U and Bagan	82
20	Nyaung-U	84
21	Mount Popa	86
22	Nyaung-U	89
23	Nyaung-U to Nyaungshwe	92
24	Nyaungshwe, Inle Lake	95
25	Nyaungshwe, Inle Lake	99
26	Nyaungshwe to Yangon	102
27	Yangon	104

Flower in the crannied wall
I pluck you out of the crannies
I hold you here, root and all, in my hand
Little flower but if I could understand
What you are, root and all, and all in all
I should know what God and man is.
                              Alfred Lord Tennyson

1

Yangon

I wake from a deep sleep thinking it must be noon to find it's not yet seven o'clock and there is time to chase a full day. A monk sits at a table talking to two people from the hostel who are going to teach English nearby and they ask if I'll join them.

Yangon is a confusion of mess and noise, shiny developments and child labourers, friendly smiles and nods amidst the chaos. Yesterday's debris has been cleared from the streets by night's vanishing cloth of darkness. Cool air soothes the gutter's foul breath, where well fed rats direct interrogating eyes at passing people in the night.

The first pagoda we pass has flaking paint and old car tyres stacked in a corner along with a sign listing exorbitant entrance fees for tourists. The citizens have a green vein, enlivening dusty streets with pot plants at every shopfront, corner or stairwell.

In the class, we choose a table each and sit as students arrive to trade questions with us. Nicole, who is learning English to try and get a different job, asks me funny questions about my love life and teaches me to do the same in Burmese. Afterwards, two of my teacher-pupils take me out for breakfast at an Indian restaurant. Nicole refuses to let me pay and I wander back to the hostel struck by her sweetness and generosity.

*

I sit anchored to the ground by the presence of the ancient Bodhi tree which this shrine has been built around. The sun shining through the octagonal roof opening brings a porcelain statue of Buddha to life. He sits in the lotus position with one hand draped towards the ground and the other tucked away. Flowers, incense and a glass of water are the only signs of the monastery's inhabitants. Through the roof, the new monastery building is set against the blue scaffolding of a modern high-rise which will soon loom over the grounds. The temple's gold base is cracked and flaking, shifting and ageing along with the sacred fig. Incense wafts around as two women administer to their faith. Splashes of water douse the hum of traffic and a cawing crow. A sporadic bell rings. Mr Ke-O passes to see how I am, and finds me well. He lives outside the grounds, while his father, a monk with eighty-six years, lives here.

The Bodhi tree curls itself up and around and into the sky, its trunk an indistinguishable mass of vines or roots all combining. In the sixty or more years since the little temple appeared, it has gently pushed away the floor and altar until they sat easier. The steadfast statue stares at me. Only the slow drift of the sun behind the tree varies its aspect. Incense leaves the shade and becomes visible, rising from the building and up the tree trunk. A breeze rises to clear the air then falls; the smoke thickens and ropes around the tree once more before being pulled up and away from the temple. I pull myself up and away and keep walking.

*

The spray of fountains into the air is bright white against the olive-green water of the lake. The golden bulk of a vast pagoda shines above the trees on the far shore. The whirring of a whipper-snipper wielded by a gardener floats over the water. Men and women in fluorescent vests work their way around the water's edge, picking out heaps of lake weed and the odd piece of rubbish, with a child in tow who grins at me as he annoys his mother. She laughs and has a smile on her face as I say, '*Min-gala-ba*. Hello.'

A young boy who rides his bike along the jetty comes to see what I'm doing. We complement the lake. Young couples sit in shared secrecy on the benches along the shore. Some kiss with no hurry while others stroll along the boardwalk with umbrellas to combat the strong sun. The only person moving fast is another tourist who walks with a heavy tread and a straight gaze. The boy washes his hands in the lake and sits next to me. We gaze over it in silence.

I farewell the boy and walk along the lake's paths before realising that he is still with me. I say goodbye again, keep walking, and he follows on his bike. Up the street we go, with him not far behind. I duck through the heavy traffic and feel a keen awkwardness in not knowing quite how to act to regain my solitude.

*

Old trees shade the cobbled entrance to the great looming spire of gold which overlooks the lake. While eating the baked nuts I bought from a woman on the railway bridge and talking to the man on the bench next to me, there is no rush to enter.

Shwedagon Pagoda is alive with people. A flock of Burmese tourists, monks, the faithful, workers and the odd foreigner circle the sacred site. Bamboo scaffolding covers the central spire, due for a touch-up. The intricate mesh preserves its curved form but masks the tower's gold brilliance. People still pose for photos in front of the clothed pagoda. Each corner of the spire's great stone base represents an astrological post designated by a day of the week. Buddhists light candles and incense at the long pedestals and Thursday Corner attracts a crowd. They pray then splash holy water over the statue sitting in a stone house. There is significance in even the smallest of details of the great structure. In each of the countless nooks and crannies is a different statue; in the eight stations of the corners is a different theme reflected in the intricate gilding and shaping of gold and stone, in every place a different message for those who know how to receive it. In a room decorated with pillars covered in brilliant gemstones of fiery ruby and sapphire, facing a statue of Buddha adorned by a halo of flashing lights, I close my eyes and breathe.

In the open, amateur photographers hassle a group of Burmese women and offer to pay them for a shot. Three monks act out ringing a bell for a young Burmese man to record on video, and a tourist jumps in front of where I stand, watching, to record his moment. Brooms scratch away the spiritual detritus of burnt wicks and windblown incense ash in Thursday Corner.

People here have a manner of delicateness which doesn't compete for space or attention. They make steady eye contact and smile as soon as I do. A young lady does just that, laughs, points me out to her friend, who too smiles and laughs as I wave, and they continue their loop of the centre. A security guard holding a cartooned plastic plate wanders by in bare feet. Middle-aged Western men walk around, alert, cameras in hand to capture all angles. Young Western men pass with their longyis knotted high above the waist and almost achieve assimilation. Thursday Corner has another bath.

*

A gold pot of burning incense sits next to an array of tables filled with candles, flowers, donation boxes and sticks of incense. People gather where the central pagoda is visible and kowtow. Some perform the movement a couple of times, some many. A woman kowtows then prepares to take a selfie. A monk sits next to me and chants in a soft tone. Children play on the legs of the marquee which shades us.

Crows shimmer black and blue in the sun as they fly among the bamboo hive of the central tower. They fall from the heights with an indistinct raggedness before catching air with their wings and gliding serene through the scaffolds to hide in their canopy of gold leaves. A long row of women circle the tower wielding two brooms each, which they criss-cross to sweep the day's dust before them.

The sun fades and brings out a rosy iridescence in the pagoda. Incandescent lights bring a new perspective, the bright gold spire's hues contrasting with the deep crow's blue of the darkening sky. Even more people than earlier mill in the central circle. I see a woman picking things off the ground with great care, and cautiously step over, worried there are animals on the ground.

She stands up and opens her hand. 'Starflower,' she says in a soft, clear voice. In her palm lies a flower, many-petalled, intricate, fragile and with the slightest hint of yellow to its whiteness.

'Pretty, right?' I say in Burmese, gathering two for myself.

*

Hung from a timber pole between thick posts polished by the years is a five-metalled bell cast by an inspired king of many generations passed. Toll the bell three times, and so spread merit to all people. There is a tangible quality of patience in those who sit in meditation here. In the midst of Yangon, this place shows a stillness in movement, a quietness in noise, a calmness in chaos. Candles flicker in flame the whole way round the pagoda. They cast a smoky haze which softens the already soft gold outer houses. A part of the place's mystique becomes clearer, for its magic is entwined with the people. It lies in the tangibility of a crowd in the scent of incense, flickering candles, the buzz of a nature that is in no way frenetic but as alive as any other. It is not static in the sense of a church with an ordered and restrained activity at certain times. This is a place of communal spirituality.

A slight man sounds the bell again and over again. I become conscious and turn to see him giving it short, measured strikes until he finds resonance. The bell rings and hums. I turn away, close my eyes and feel the bell's vibration throughout my body. The strikes stop and the final humming continues, ebbing until I open my eyes anew. It is a bell of consciousness.

In a pram a blond-haired French boy wonders at the bell, at the buildings, at all things. His little brother rounds the corner, reaches the top and exclaims his delight in the marvel he faces. His tired father takes him away to keep him quiet for those meditating. The toddler feels the pull of the place and squeals in protest.

*

On the lower terraces which lead to the pagoda's raised base are gardens fashioned from hundreds of potted plants. Long rows of the same plant in the same pot, rich purple foliage in burnt-red ceramics, set against rows of contrasting plants with their own pots have a hypnotic effect. To walk along the stone paths of the lowest terrace to the highest is to walk through a garden of incredible mobile richness. I walk a final loop of the pagoda with feet worn and warmed by the stone which the feet of so many have walked smooth. I glance up to meet the painted black eyes of a woman lying on her side. Her serene face rests in her palm and I realise that it was under her gaze that I first sat, to write and let go of the need to see all there is to see, so many rich hours ago.

Over the course of a day, spiritual and communal acts mount, their physical remnants scattered on the stone and swept away many times, their intangible weight building until late at night it is as if the very stones exhale peace. The temple is ancient, and each transient day's action joins a store many centuries old. Only the crows could know who has remained constant in their interactions with this place since it was built to house eight hairs from the head of Gautama Buddha himself.

*

A young man leads me through the vast symmetrical grounds to the southernmost of the four long corridors which will give me the heading home. People crouch by piles of vegetables, slicing them into boiling pots, as they prepare for a holy festival which begins before sunrise. At the main entrance, where the loud babble of hawkers chased me into the temple at midday, I am farewelled with the silent industry of closing time.

2

Yangon to Ngwesaung

Up early to duck into the cool freshness of morning, the sun already promising heat. I turn the first corner to find a calm side street. Lush plants with dampness still upon them line the footpaths and groups of people sit on small red stools and eat steaming hot rice with cups of tea. I pull up a stool and wolf down a plate of garlic rice and a fried egg. I ask if I can have some tea and they pass the pot over.

With a full belly and content with the ease of it, I wander along admiring the plants until I hear a clear ringing tone. A train of young monks led by an elder and a man without the saffron robes approach. The man holds a bronze gong in front of his brow and strikes it with a wooden mallet. They collect alms of money or food which the street's residents tip from their small bowls into the head monk's tall tin pot. As they tread past, a few of the boys look over and return my smile.

A few minutes behind, a hunched woman in saffron passes, bearing a silver bowl and chanting in a strong, old voice. She places one careful foot in front of the other, her heels slipping out of the sandals, yet seems invisible in the footsteps of the boys.

*

To go to Pathein, I hop on a packed local bus which will take me to a depot on the outskirts of Yangon. Huddled up with my pack on my lap, I look in fascination at a city passing by. I look at the quantity of traffic, the people in the street, the road building, the myriad shop signs with English and Burmese script, at mysterious gardens behind steel bars, at contrasting sights in every direction which change with the passing of the dusty air to keep us cool.

Two hours later, my half-panicked questions meet brief assurances before the bus leaves and I stand on a busy roadside with no hint of another bus. Following pointed arms a short walk up a dirt road is the depot. I plonk myself on a plastic easy chair next to a shallow dam, ticket to Pathein in hand, and half an hour vanishes.

*

Arctic air and electro-pop from a television blast the bus. The TV has as much adhesive power for the locals as the curiosities of the world outside have for me. Pathein is two hundred kilometres west of Yangon and the more I look at the map the more I realise how big the country is. The coast seems a distant possibility.

I wake in the countryside with the odd cow and a pair of buffalo in flat rice fields. The bus swerves around potholes and bumps. Rickety wooden footbridges cross the stagnant water of the roadside channel, food stalls and huts punctuate the verge and rice paddies cover the plains. In a basket on top of a man's head, boiled shrimp sweat in the afternoon heat. Corn husks and plastic bottles litter the kerb. I share pieces of roast plantain with the young man next to me.

The bus moves deeper into rural Myanmar, and with a strength of curiosity in every hut, every face, every scrounging pig and mangy dog which line the roads question piles upon question as I look and wonder at what I see. Farmers crouch in the water feeling around in the mud, bamboo and palm thatch sheds grow mysteries, pumpkin-like vines grow along grapevine-like trellises, flowers adorn the bonnets of tractors and, for all that, I wonder at what I don't see, with an absent police presence.

The bus pulls up to an open-air food hall and I try to find out how long we'll stay. I watch the crowd of people sitting at square wooden tables, sip on a coffee, stretch out my legs, look out over the dirt car park and the unfamiliar land of dusty lushness and feel a sudden joy.

At the depot in Pathein, I find I've missed the last bus to Ngwesaung by an hour, and to Chaungtha by a few minutes. A group of men jostle for my fare as I ask about my options. Eager to keep moving and see the coast, I take a scooter driver's high price of 15,000 kyat to go to Ngwesaung.

From the back of the scooter, I exchange waves with people, get closer to all the sights of the bus, hear better the sounds, smell the scents and feel the warm afternoon air on my face as my pilot adroitly navigates the curves, the road and traffic of all description. When we break sixty on a good downhill stretch, tears squeeze themselves out of the corners of my eyes. Once we face into the steady sea breeze, the taste of salt in the air, I give up holding onto my huge helmet and let it hang back on my head. At a tiny shop along the road, as the driver puts air into the tyres, I joke with the woman about tigers in the jungle. '*Zakheer*,' she says as I pretend to be one, reminding me of Kipling's Shere Khan. The two-hour ride is one of fascination, is energising and joyful, and we arrive in Ngwesaung at sundown.

*

Hopes of finding a room and seeing the sunset dissolve in the reality that finding a room in Myanmar is not simple. Most guest houses are only for locals and there are no hostels here. I wind up in a Four Seasons Hotel for more than I budgeted – about the opposite of what I envisioned after Yangon. Yet the beach is calm, the air warm with a soft breeze, the people smiling, and the promise of dinner and a beer awaits. I sit on the beach writing by the bright spotlight of a resort. Four people on scooters come up and try to sell me a firework which they will set off on the spot. We have some banter and part ways. It's very quiet here – the opposite to Yangon's main roads. My stomach rumbles.

As I walk back along the beach in the dark, a man nears from behind me. I grip my torch in my pocket with a sense of paranoia before stopping, pretending to have a drink, so he goes ahead. '*Mingalaba*,' he says as he passes, nodding.

My waiter, Aung Aung, and I trade laughs as I write and eat *tatalo-saa-me* before the restaurant quietens and he makes my table our table, sitting for a long time chatting, as he teaches me more phrases and fixes my pronunciation. He invites me for coffee tomorrow morning and I return to the hotel with a light heart.

3

Ngwesaung to Chaungtha

In the early morning, I am vague and aimless, knowing only that I should eat before meeting Aung Aung at nine. In the dining room is a man called Jack who travels the country selling defibrillators. Twenty minutes after taking my map over to his table, he fills me with enthusiasm to see the places he says I must see and take the routes he says I must not take, describing the trip from here to the far north coast as very difficult for locals and impossible for foreigners. Before I go, he tells me some of the country's fraught history with a hopeful tone.

*

Aung Aung meets me outside the restaurant and we greet each other with a laugh. In the shop across the street, we drink strong black coffee with a slice of lime squeezed in. He teaches me Burmese by naming everything in the shop and the lizards on the ceiling, *amyau*. I write down everything he says in my little notebook and repeat it until I've got it right, practising with him and the people in the shop, who look on as I mangle their language.

We move to useful phrases. 'First time in Myanmar', 'I am crazy', and on it goes, the onlookers laughing at the moment I finally get the tone right and become intelligible. I scratch them into my book as fast as I can and enjoy the bittersweet flavour of lime and sugar in the coffee grounds. He is completely at ease with the bizarreness we present to the locals and the two hours he has before returning to work end too soon.

In the hotel, I ponder my direction before packing, checking out and leaving my bag behind to walk to the beach. The sun is hot and the walk through dusty streets takes me far enough to long for the water. I run and dive into the Bay of Bengal, swimming away from the shore underwater until my lungs are bursting, then come up for air to surface and float with an incredible freeness on my back, look up at the sky, feel the warm water on my body and for a moment question my reality. The little stresses wash away and I'm left with joy, to be travelling again and to meet someone like Aung Aung. I am invigorated.

I bob about in the water catching small white caps and shore-breaking waves before drying off and walking towards the point. The sun is glorious on my back in the cool breeze and my legs begin to run of their own accord. I settle into an easy rhythm, sucking in lungfuls of fresh air, and splash into the water at the point. I walk back drying off with the sun on my face and feel ready to move.

*

Over another variety of *tatalo-saa-me*, I exchange jokes with Aung Aung, who helps me flirt with one of the waitresses. Her sister looks on in amusement. The double serve of rice and fresh vegetables is exhaustingly good and even though I could sit at the table for hour after hour, the time to leave arrives. Aung Aung and I hug, exchange good wishes, and I hop on the back of the scooter to be caught by surprise when it takes off and a sudden sadness rises within me, in the instantaneous recognition of having made a friend at the moment of departure.

*

The road of dirt, rocks and potholes winds into low hilly jungle towards Chaungtha. We pass a couple of tourists sharing a scooter to

Ngwesaung. The driver turns and tells me the name of each village we enter, before we come to open fields bordered by palm jungle. Brahman cattle tethered to tall bamboo poles graze in circles. Tall palms shade the villages, towering over the huts and bungalows. Some are great double-storey constructions with open-air windows and palm leaf thatching, others have shiny blue tin roofs. Pigs tethered to short stakes root through the jungle floor. I sit relaxed on the scooter with both hands free and wave, smile and *mingalaba* to dozens of villagers and passers-by. Their faces crack open to show huge smiles, some with red-juice-covered teeth. Some wave, some smile and nod, and only a very few are too caught in thought or unwilling to give any response at all.

We pass a little industry, a coconut-husking mill and the distinct smell of a shrimp farm, before re-entering the jungle.

The familiar sounds of screaming and yelling children come from a small primary school in a village. We keep going and arrive at the water's edge for a boat crossing. After the closeness of the jungle road, the clear width of the river is disorienting. The driver eases the scooter up a plank of wood and the ferryman pushes us into the current, slides up the ramp and climbs in to manoeuvre the rudder – the motor's rotor on a long axle – and get us underway. I stand at the prow, looking at the jungle across the turbulent dirty blue water, wondering at the mysteries upriver as it weaves through the mangroves and grinning as I remember a scene from *Fitzcarraldo* of jungle daring and adventure.

We disembark, drive through a toll booth – a palm shelter with a stick over a rock – and glide through a quiet stretch until reaching the second crossing. We wait next to the veranda of a hut with two cross-legged Burmese women talking behind us. Their voices are steady and smooth, rising and falling in a narrow band. Small pigs run in and out from under the house and a young pup, a hazel-coated bundle of fuzzy independence, trots past ignoring my whistle. A boy of three or four amuses himself, working on a construction of impressive imagination.

I ask permission to wander and find three rotund sows tethered behind the house. My pilot says they are four years old, and for pork and rice when I make a throat-slitting motion. Next to the veranda the piglets emerge, rooting at the find of a fresh young palm shoot. The biggest, a stout black pig, waggles its tail back and forth in delight. The smaller mottled pigs nose around the palm shoot in a bunch, one nuzzling at my bootlaces in confusion. I take a seat, legs dangling, and the pup comes by playing with a stick.

The boy keeps building, using a pole, a fishing net, a tricycle wheel and some palm stalks to engineer magic. The pigs nose the shoot into the wheel of the scooter, and the moment I reach for the camera the boy runs in brandishing a stick, the pigs flee and the scene becomes a memory.

We set off from the mangroves, the boy pointing the way, with a dour pilot who pushes the boat off before I've finished taking off my boots. 'Wait wait wait,' I say as he ignores me, and splash aboard.

Over the river, a clear beach greets us, a jungle highway. We speed along with surf breaking against rocks on our left, tall palms on our right and wind and sun blowing through our hair.

At the third crossing, the boat, already half-full of people and goods, docks at the same modest jetty as a huge luxury speedboat. '*Mingalaba*,' I say to the other passengers. I try to buy one banana from an elderly woman on board but she wants to sell the whole bunch. I try to explain I have a stomach only so big and am full of *tatalo-saa-me* and manage to offend her before spending the rest of the crossing in silence.

*

Chaungtha is a large tourist town whose outskirts make the paradisiacal perfection of Ngwesaung clear. The roadside is filthy and the first guest house we stop at doesn't accept foreigners. They mention an expensive hotel and my expectations again result in disappointment. The driver calls his brother, who recommends the Sea & See guest house. In the courtyard outside the modest pink building, where they ask $10 a night for an airy room with a bed covered in children's cartoon blankets and a fan, my flattened expectations become a hypocritical source of great joy. Tyu Tyu is the host. She is warm, friendly and makes me feel settled. We chat for a while before I go walking.

A fresh westerly whips the Bay of Bengal into a churning mass of white caps as the orange sun-ball penetrates the subcontinental haze. Pagoda Rock sits, impassive, on the northern point of Chaungtha Beach. From afar it appears a pile of rubble, and from near a piece of architecture in the style of Machu Picchu; a smooth chamber surrounded by rough-hewn rock close to its original form.

Groups of Burmese and Chinese tourists gather along the beach. Many play football between goals of coconuts or sandals stuck on sticks. Burmese girls ride past on bicycles. A boy sits, feet out to sea and arms to the sides in a position of repose as the shoals wash over his legs. Men towing food stalls on tricycles peddle skewers of mysterious meat which a family behind me feast on. The sun becomes bold orange as it drops through the haze. As it nears the horizon, two birds take off from Pagoda Rock, where a blue box kite and a hardy shrub flutter next to each other. The guest houses facing the beach sit empty after weathering the peak of the holiday season.

*

The power comes back on as I open the diary to see if it's too dark to write. A mosquito coil burns by my feet on a slanted bench made for relaxed attitudes in the courtyard of the guest house. Tyu Tyu comes and goes in a brilliant green and turquoise longyi.

*

The restaurant has inviting coloured light bulbs strung up around the yard. I choose a table near a group of young men and sit down before realising how drunk they are. They surround a table full of empty whisky and beer bottles and I should leave, but the men are keen to talk, so I stay. The unpredictability of their drunken stupor makes me uneasy and sharp. I praise the food cooked by a man who barely controls a slur. I praise the country, the women and them. We talk football and I keep an eye on the drunkest man, whose laughter follows the others and never comes to his eyes. I finish my beer, pay and say goodbye, walking further down the road with a clear-headed confidence.

*

On the return I slide past the restaurant and buy a bottle of beer from the neighbouring shop. The power is out so I light the coil and sit in darkness on the bench, listening to scooters fly past, the odd firework go off and the growing night. Tyu Tyu and others return and as she stands behind the counter inside with a candle lit, I sing to myself. A little girl arrives later and they go to bed. I pour the last glass of beer into a flower pot and let the night claim me.

4

Chaungtha

The concrete white and glass-blue block of Hotel Ace sits high up on the northern point, visible from the whole beach. It looks unoccupied. The Caribbean-themed pirate ship restaurant at its base needs a coat of paint, and toppled benches dot the deck. On the other side of the bridge is a broken barbed-wire fence and a thatched hut by the roadside. I sneak in and at the edge of the estuary rapid movements catch my eye. There are mudskippers all over the banks, curious crawling and jumping creatures I've only seen on one of David Attenborough's series before. I wander past the hut and see I'm not the first visitor here. Conscious that from the road I must look like I'm finding a place to crap, I retreat to the bridge and sit on the bank with my towel over my head to ward off the sun. The creatures hop and wiggle their way around, disregarding the heaps of rubbish banked in the water or the excrement which will soon wash in. Attenborough's lot were in a much cleaner area from what I could see.

Over the other side of a high concrete wall ten metres away, workers water plush lawns and manicured palms. Up the street, the mangroves deteriorate and gather mounds of plastic. The smell of stagnant, dirty water with a hint of sewage, which grows more familiar, floats over the road. A renewable energy farm lies untended as diesel generators clatter away in sheds outside hotels. The wind turbine's blades are still and the solar panels have a thick coating of dust, a growth of vines. Two dogs stand alert at the fence line before bounding away through the panels to the far corner.

Single-cylinder engines attached to four-wheeled carts make

rudimentary utes. They clack along with singular explosions of noise as their drivers ease them over the bridge deck. Clack – clack – clack – clack – clack – and on again. In the courtyard of the guest house, a gecko splays itself on the wall. Its tail has fallen off, leaving a dark pink stump. I am so close I can see its tiny toes, with one sharp little claw each, and I lean in closer in fascination. When my face is inches away, it darts off, startling me for fairness's sake.

*

Enlivened by the swim and the exploring, I pass time at the guest house getting to know the young man who appeared last night. Tehnai-tho is sixteen, tall and slim with large, elegant feet and hands. He has short black hair artfully styled and a smile which is quick to emerge. His eyes are bright and he tends towards pensiveness after frenetic noise and laughter. Ready to go to school, he wears a crisp white short-sleeved shirt and a dark green longyi. A thick gold ring adorns his wedding finger as it would be at home. He talks in quick, even tones, except when he repeats what is for him a basic phrase. He advances and puts forth syllables in a slow deep voice as if for a naughty child. Then he laughs and says the whole phrase as fast as he can until my tongue splutters in repetition.

Tyu Tyu says hello from the open windows with a smile. She is wearing bright pink and on her cheeks has painted small squares of *thanaka*, a yellow paste made from tree bark. There is a pink brooch in her hair, which is black and tinted gold and hides a smudged birthmark on her right cheek. She teaches me Burmese too with the help of her English as I write more phrases and practise what Aung Aung taught me. I cross out and rewrite phonetic scribbles as I struggle to come to grips with the finesse of the language's tones.

*

A family sort coconuts in the front yard of their small thatched hut. The mother squats, watching, with a curved machete in hand. The son shifts stray coconuts into the corner while the father heaves them over the fence onto a big pile next to a waiting truck.

A foreigner sits watching at the base of a palm tree. He shifts most of the pile over the fence, and mother and a younger child move to sit on the edge of the hut. As he is busy moving the pile, the foreigner walks around the side of the truck and says something unintelligible. He gestures to the coconuts and picks one up before throwing it in the tray, saying 'Yes?'

The family laugh and the two men start hurling them in until the pile is gone. When the stranger throws one too gently, it bounces off the tray and hits the farmer's hand.

'Sorry, sorry, sorry,' he says.

The farmer laughs again. '*Ya-ba-de*. No problem.'

The pile is gone. They exchange a few words in different tongues before he leaves and asks to take a photo. The man returns to write under the palm tree and the farmer returns to his yard to shift another pile over the fence.

The hut is timber with a palm and bamboo pole roof. It is four metres square and the roof slopes one way. From the veranda you see dotted palms amidst dry brown grass and green creeping ivy which covers coarse white sand. Past the palms and bright green mangroves lies the flat grey-blue of the Bay of Bengal. On a bamboo shelter off a path to the beach, a sheet of betel nuts dries in the sun, anchored by split coconuts. A bus width of road passes the hut through dust and sand.

Another child emerges from the hut, a little girl in a sky-blue dress with the clay-like *thanaka* coating her face. The young boy wears Myanmar colours, red shorts and green T-shirt, and also has his face painted in the earthy yellow shade. The air is clean and full. The westerly takes the bite out of the sun in gentle gusts. They call this the cold season. The young boy and his little sister walk to the shelter and back towing a sled made out of half a plastic jerrycan. When the boy finds a whole plastic bag, he tosses it to catch the wind like a balloon. He smiles at the strange man from a distance, hiding behind a palm tree when the man smiles back at him for too long.

The farmer finishes loading the truck and toots his horn to get the stranger's attention. The stranger looks up and the farmer waves and smiles before getting in with his eldest son and driving north, waving again as he goes. The mother yells out and the little girl runs over to help her brother move a good-sized palm log. She can't lift it but manages to drag it back so the boy can put it on the other side of the tree. A dog noses around the scrub with the beautiful dingo-coloured coat common here. It is thin but not mangy like those of Yangon.

A scooter with two men on it stops outside the hut. A monk hops off holding a plastic drum of red liquid then returns. They continue north. Another dog appears, a bitch with sagging underbelly.

Behind the hut is a small clearing, an untended outhouse and then bush. A steep hillock shrouded in vines, bamboo and banana trees shoots out of the ground.

The boy hoists a ten-litre drum of water onto his shoulder and stutters away from the hut. He comes back with a wet patch down his back. He keeps picking through the scrub and builds a stack of firewood out of palm leaf stems. The little girl plays with the lower reaches of a mangrove. She collects a handful of things and tosses them over her shoulder as she goes. The boy has enough wood and finds kindling, crumpling it in his hands.

The palms stand tall and skinny and gentle in the light wind, only the fronds, suspended from long stems, bobbing in slow motion. Coconuts sit in the bowl of the tree, green and small and big and orange. The trunks are reddish-brown and worn as if they are often climbed. Others are lighter grey.

The father and eldest son are still away. The rest of the family gather in the hut. The young boy comes out with a bowl of food and sits on the veranda to eat.

The sea rolls onto the shore with a steady rhythm. Palm leaves rustle against each other and a scooter with three men on it putters by.

The stranger at the base of the tree gets up and waves goodbye.

*

Walking back under the setting sun, I see beauty where I've never looked before. It is in the patterns on the sand formed by water flowing back to the sea, in the chaotic tracks of spiral-shelled creatures, in the curve of readiness small fish keep in their bodies after a shadow on their rock pool frightens them, in the pink shades of sand and rock in the gentle afternoon sun; and it is in the palm trunks which glow in the soft light.

Teh-nai-tho drives me home along the beach. At the guest house I meet A-tho, a family friend who has gregarious, loud laughter which contrasts with the dry, quiet manner of Tyu Tyu's uncle, U-le. She watches from behind the counter as A-tho, U-le and two of the three brothers drink, talk and tease each other around the coffee table. I flip my little notebook's pages and they marvel at my inability to get the tones right. When they leave late at night, I join her and U-le at the gate, standing still and looking to the road. Teh-nai-tho comes back on the scooter with the little girl.

5

Chaungtha

The screaming joy of Burmese tourists rises over the sound of waves crashing onto the beach and washing the shore of its footprints. People bob in inflated truck tyre tubes, wearing all their clothes and the breaking waves on their heads. I dive into the water, stroking through the wash and bodysurf into the shore and back, over and over again. Their joy is potent and infectious as they wonder at the ocean and drift in and out of a sense of security where their feet can touch the ground.

I tow in a group of girls who have gone too far to make it in without a struggle. We laugh together before I swim back out to glide down the face of the warm two-foot waves before riding the whitewash with one arm out in front of my face. When I swim out the back to float under the clear blue sky, the whistles of the lifeguards sound to call me in.

On the beach, I dry off in the sun before walking back to the guest house to meet Teh-nai-tho, who has invited me to join his family for lunch.

*

The family live in a beautiful hut on a slope overlooking a dam and a couple of fields about a kilometre out of town. The father sits cross-legged on the floor next to a teapot and cups. I greet them and sit cross-legged with father and son. We have a banana each. Lunch is ready on a round low table in the centre of the hut. His mother places out a huge bowl of rice, three dishes of sautéed vegetables and a large metal bowl each. I paw food into my mouth while they roll neat balls of rice and vegetables and flick them into their mouths with their thumbs.

After lunch we sit and have tea and another banana. The father smokes a fat rolled cigarette. The family's puppy comes in and gnaws at my hand, two-month-old teeth doing no more than tickle. The hut is airy and peaceful. It is beautiful and I don't have enough compliments in Burmese. We leave and I take a photo of the family in front of the Buddhist altar. The father shows me their most treasured possession – an exquisite, shining gold-encrusted ball in a glass case.

As Teh-nai-tho and I roll down the hill past the dam and the banana palms, I am filled with a deep, happy gratitude for the kindness of the people I meet.

*

At the guest house, we sit together as Tyu Tyu has her lunch, which we brought over in steel containers. An Austrian who is also called Leo arrives to a courtyard flooded with the warmth of the noon sun and our relaxed happiness. We dub him 'Leo Hniq, Leo Two', and I tell him he's found the best guesthouse in Chaungtha without needing to see any other.

*

In the late afternoon with the sun retreating, Teh-nai-tho drives his younger brother and me to A-tho's home on Sri-Thy beach for dinner with his family. We eat and laugh and enjoy each other's company as the sun sets over the bay in a state of grace. A-tho's little girls laugh and giggle at the stranger who can't eat with his hands.

The people I meet appreciate the beauty of their surroundings, each other and life itself in a way which makes them rich beyond imagination. Life is rich, and there's no rush to live it.

The three of us fly along, me in the middle between Teh-nai-tho and his brother, the two of them singing a Burmese song. They yell out phrases for me to repeat before we all sing together, riding fast through the night light, the palms and the long smooth beach.

6

Chaungtha

I enjoy lying in my cocoon of blankets and mosquito netting listening to the morning. Well before dawn, roosters crow in choking cries which won't get their heads lopped off. The light strengthens and I wake from a second slumber to see palm fronds waving on the back of my door and blue sky peeping through the gap in the curtains. Scooters and tractor carts pass on the main road but their horns are quiet until the day has begun in earnest. Sparrows chatter from a tree by the road and in the distance a crow caws. Men's voices cry out greetings and jibes. Laughter rings out and the front door to the house opens. Teh-nai-tho comes in half singing something in search of Tyu Tyu before falling quiet when he sees no sign of life.

*

The surf at Chaungtha beach washes away the mental cobwebs which build with a morning in bed and the sense of the day passing by regardless of your attendance. There are fewer people in the surf but I dive in and catch waves to get my blood flowing. On the beach, a group of football players ask for a photo and I put down my towel and a big smile grows with theirs. One player has his longyi rolled down to show the designer label of his underwear – they are Kalen Kelun's. They are fresh from finishing a tournament and drink Myanmar beers and laugh as they horse around in the sand and the shallows.

*

Leo is sitting outside the hostel in the sun. I mention the scooter to him and he's keen but has a tummy bug, so we pass time in the courtyard before he decides he's ready. Tyu Tyu offers us the use of their scooter but I worry about any accidents and decide on a rental. There is no way to communicate my reasons for rejecting their kindness.

The man at the store rents a scooter with one condition: 'Return it the way you found it.'

The route out of town follows yesterday's trip and we take off with Leo's long legs sticking out to the sides and his weight wobbly behind me. At the beach, the tide is out and the dry sand moves under us, shifting and grabbing at the wheels. Leo jumps off to avoid a fall as I wrestle with the handlebars. He leaps free often enough that I'm glad we didn't use the family's. The sun has a sting that makes the distant palms at the end of the bay all the more inviting. It is sheer relief to make their shade and the easier going of the dusty paths, where we putter along between the slender trunks, bouncing over the bumps and settling into a smoother rhythm.

*

Timber slat canoes bob in the emerald shallows of an estuary to the bay. A boat with bamboo poles shooting from its deck edges towards the shore with two fishermen in caps on board. From the village on the far shore, the strains of megaphonic music carry over on the wind. A pagoda's red-roofed tower rises from the trees and palm huts huddle on the shore. At the river mouth, the palm jungle is unimpeded by buildings and stands thick to the shore, its cool dark depths a sanctaury from the noon sun. The breeze chops up the water and laps onto the shore, cooling the air. The ferry putters across.

*

Leo and I sit in the shade opposite the steady attention of four men. I scratch away in my journal when the ferry arrives and I realise I have to ride the scooter on board. I rev it up the plank without wobbling off the side and relax.

We scoot through the sun, the palms and their shade, flickering in and out of darkness until the afternoon is halfway to evening and the fuel tank halfway to empty. We ride through the small town on the other side of the river and keep our eyes peeled for a chance to venture off the road.

Not far from town, the huts give way to long uninterrupted stretches of palms. When we spot a track to the beach, we take it, Leo hopping off as I churn through fine dust and sand to pull up at an abandoned shack. On the other side of the palms is a beach like none I've seen before. The fine sand is bright white, the water a thin turquoise and not a person or building breaks the gentle arc of the bay as it reaches north and south along its border of green-fronded palms. The water rises and falls as clean waves roll through it towards us. We laugh in disbelief, amazed at our sudden isolation in paradise.

As we swim through the warm water, we are children, laughing, splashing and throwing ourselves into the coming waves. We turn, glide and tumble into shore before running back into the depths, stepping high out of the water before falling and swimming further.

On the shore, we walk with the curiosity which a sense of beauty brings, looking under palm fronds and coconut husks for crab holes and scaring the translucent white creatures into the shadows. The sand carries their tracks and the flotsam of the bay. Pieces of cuttlefish, driftwood and long conical shells of every earthy colour imaginable scatter the shore. A pile of the giant shells grows out of our excitement. We choose one each to mark the occasion and let the sea reclaim the rest.

The thought of the last boat back over the river finally drives us home. I fantasise of a life here as we cruise south to the hostel, both of us enjoying the cooling air of late afternoon and the tranquillity which follows the exquisite sensation of the sea upon your skin and warm sand under your feet.

*

In Chaungtha, the sun falls from under a layer of cloud and promises to paint us a bright sunset for the first time since arriving here. It lands between a set of bamboo goals where boys play football before being swallowed by the night. Leo and I eat in a beachside restaurant and then meet Teh-nai-tho, A-tho, U-le and Tyu Tyu at the guest house for a farewell night of merrymaking. We drink whiskey and beer and laugh over and over at each other, at ourselves and at our garbled Burmese.

7

Chaungtha to Pathein, Ngathaingehaun and Gwa

Fighting back tears, I haul myself up into the bus over an ice box blocking the entrance. It takes a moment to work out if this is the luggage or passenger entrance, before I realise it's both. I scramble to the back corner, push the curtain aside long enough to wave goodbye as the bus takes off and bucks my pack from the windowsill. I secure it and seconds later it falls again. The woman next to me helps cram it beside the seat and I settle in with my face full of emotion. A warm and generous lady next to me and her two friends smile, make me feel comfortable and give me a lolly.

The bus lurches around on the rock and dirt road. There are five of us on the back seat and at my feet is a huge bag filled with plastic bottles. After a quarter hour's chat, the middle woman of the three, sitting on the ice box, lies on top of the bag of plastic and goes to sleep, bouncing around with the road. We wind through the jungle on a road which will join the broader one I came along from Pathein to Ngwesaung.

*

In Pathein, I struggle to find the next bus and a toilet until a local indicates the latter, a fetid watercourse. A stall sells steamed noodles for a late breakfast, my stomach and head reeling in Chaungtha in the dreary early morning. I sit next to the stall scoffing noodles when a bald man approaches, speaks Burmese to the owner and looks under the lids of the pots on the gas burners. His name is Renato and he becomes the most travelled person I've met, travelling being his way of life for half the year for the last thirty-odd. We board a crowded bus and begin the next leg of the trip up the coast.

*

We sit on a bench at the junction of two roads with our packs and the vague promise of a bus to continue on. Scooters and trucks hurry through with blaring horns. The roadside stall sells motor oil in Grand Royal Whiskey bottles from a wooden rack. Renato mentions the police, and points out two within eyeshot. They are almost all in plain clothes and I realise the truth of their conspicuous absence on the trip so far.

Renato chats with a scooter driver in search of an alternative route to Gwa. Observation halts as he suggests we try and hitch a ride on a truck after we hear the bus is five hours away. We walk along the road and over a long bridge to pass the police checkpoints and avoid trouble for a local driver. There, a car takes us over steep and winding mountain roads to Gwa. Renato and I talk on and off about our countries and our lives as we are spoilt by views that go on forever. High in the mountains at the checkpoint to Rakhine State, the police take their time over our documents. We wait outside the office, looking over the dirt road and a few pigs to the rich green ranges, far from the tourist route.

Two and a half hours later, outside the Royal Rose Guest House in Gwa, the car's driver argues with us over the fare. He grows more and more upset in the face of our insistence on the agreed amount before thrusting his hand into my chest. Renato cuts in with authority, telling me to walk away with him. You must set your boundaries, he says, when you are travelling alone.

He has a curious and fascinating way with people. He asks more of them than most would be comfortable to, with a manner of lightness and humour, and in return he receives a certain respect and a closer look at life. We share a room in the Royal Rose where cigarette butts litter the shower recess and the sink falls off the wall if you put anything heavier than a bar of soap on it.

A group of women chant without pause in a building next door. Their girls are learning the chants. The noise rises and falls, one leader's voice carrying over the rest. Cicadas back the chorus outside. After a long day of travel, emotion and stomach upsets, I am halfway to the place Jack said tourists could not reach.

8

Gwa to Linn Thar

My energy deserts me overnight. I'm left with a sore throat and tired legs. The early morning coolness is restful as I sit outside on a wide-armed wooden chair waiting to see if Renato arrives before having breakfast. We go to Ngapali at ten.

The veranda looks onto a grassy yard hemmed with pink, spindly potted plants and dark purple shrubs. Half a dozen leafy trees keep the sun out. The guest house for locals is a faded blue, and wooden window shutters open to make dusty holes in the house's face. The rusty tin roof separates the clear blue sky from the blue wall. When the sun hits the side of the house, another tone of blue jumps out. The trees wait another four months for rain, dusty and tiring even in the Burmese winter. Cicadas drone on, softer without the heavy blanket of night to sharpen the ears. Schoolchildren replace last night's women with repetitious chanting which follows the teacher.

A dirt and stone path curves past the house from the road. A cane washing basket sits empty at the base of a tree next to an upturned ceramic pot. My stomach gurgles. With no sign of Renato, I cross the road to explore the market. The long shady stalls run in some kind of order, pots and pans to clothing to plastic to vegetables and, out in the sun, to piles of fish spread on blue tarpaulins.

*

The bus is a mysterious beast. Due at ten according to everyone we spoke to last night and this morning, obliterated from their collective consciousness. No one has any idea of where we could buy a ticket to Ngapali. On our third or fourth visit to the same shop, we hear the bus might be at three because it comes all the way from Yangon. I trail Renato around town as he searches for a ride until we stumble upon a group of three people putting up advertising posters at a store for their truckload of goods. With his long arms, Renato reaches the eaves, staples them in place and becomes useful. He works fast and soon earns us a lift.

Our ride to Ngapali is a three-tonne truck carrying Tic-Tacs and Wasuka water. A young Chinese woman brandishing seaweed-flavour tics or tacs emblazons the side. Renato squeezes into the middle between the driver and his two companions and I hop into the two-foot-wide recess behind the seat, sitting cross-legged with my head grazing the roof as Renato tries not to get in the way of the gearstick.

We stop at every village which has a small shop along the way and look at the rural heart of western Myanmar between. The first shock of seeing the biting labour of the men and women working to construct a bitumen road comes as we round a bend and stop. Fires burn under smoking barrels of tar, choking dust swirls in the heat and women cart plastic baskets of rock and gravel, sorted and loaded with bare hands, to pour onto the reeking surface. Their faces are stern and those of Chaungtha's coastal contentment and easy smiles feel distant.

In the fields, tall Brahman cattle pull carts of hay to roughly shaped stacks. In a village, a youth cuts wood into pieces to stoke a hot circle of fire to heat a belt of steel to fit a cart's wheel. The farmer talks of the work in rapid Burmese and we nod in unison. We cross rivers of clear green water with palms growing like mangroves in the shallows. I chew a betel-nut wrapped in a leaf and spend the next ten minutes spitting grainy red fragments into a bottle, reassuring the excited co-pilot that no, I am not dizzy.

He shows me strings of the betel fruit, nuts within, drying on the second floor railing of a wooden house and the betel tree kept for the home, a thin type of palm. 'If you have enough,' he says, 'you will go to paradise!'

Over lunch, a six-year-old boy serves us, eager to show off his ability. He says thank you in confident English and Renato plays with him as he comes and goes. Renato asks if he goes to school and finds he's home-schooled due to the distance.

We go on and I snooze in the back, braced between the wall and jerrycans of fuel. The journey of eighty miles takes us six hours. When Ngapali arrives, their guest house, a small one with the most well looked after, tasteful garden I've seen, turns us away. We farewell the three and go on foot. As at Ngwesaung, hopes of a swim at sunset fade with it as we struggle to find a cheap guest house with a licence to accept foreigners. Our sense of exploratory independence wanes and we use the tip Renato got from a Frenchwoman for the SMS guest house in Linn Thar village. Rene and I are keen for adventure and hire bikes to ride into Ngapali. We wander around a 200-dollar a night resort and I nearly topple into the central pool before he grabs me by the shirt.

In the dimness of the hostel, I write in an old dining room. It has wooden floorboards and long walls with only a lonely desk, table and an upholstered chair to furnish it. The chair is an exquisite antique with an attached side table, perfect for writing. It is simple, yet fine, curved and straight, comfortable and useful. A rat scurries around the edges of the room and the soft laughter of the French couple we met earlier carries through the thin walls. A man sings from the distant road. The night murmurs in winter's heat.

9

Linn Thar

I wake in the morning when Renato gets up then snooze on. My nine a.m. alarm startles me, for the windowless room is pitch-black and timeless. Over a coffee and breakfast, I flip through state maps and see a land fractured by mountains, valleys and rivers. The date becomes confusing. It excites Renato to speak French again and he talks with the couple we met for a moment last night. His boisterousness draws a reluctant smile from the solemn owner.

*

Renato and I ride bicycles through and beyond the wealth of Ngapali's centre and into the poorer fishing village to the south. We stop at a Buddhist monastic school where the children run ragged on an area bare of grass next to a deep dam of stagnant green water. As the lunch break ends, the head monk tells us and the teacher to tour the building rather than bother him and the other fourteen monks who live here. As he gives us the full tour, the teacher's pride shines. The schoolhouse is a beautiful white building, four storeys high with gilt caves and lime-green pillars. The classes run on the first and second floors; on the third is a beautiful library smelling of books, polish and still air. The fourth opens to the rooftop with a pagoda, a shrine and a view of the palms and neighbouring village. We see the children taking classes who gaze at us and we leave before causing too much of a disruption to their day.

Further through the village, we stop to eat and drink thin-skinned bananas, avocados and sickly sweet iced coffees and milk. The younger sister of the lady running the shop is very pretty and I compliment her, '*A lo hlare.*'

The father and two sisters laugh. She has a boyfriend, so I show my heart breaking. I ask to buy a bottle of water and they give me one as a present.

*

Riding south, we turn off the main road which curves into the jungle and come to a cove full of fishing craft and lined with palms, beached boats and huts. A swimmable distance off the rocky shore is White Sands Island and a line of palm-leaf umbrellas. Two little girls, one in the white and green school dress and the other with undercut hair, a purple dress and two big gold earrings, watch us. Renato goes along in their steps until they stop at a sand pile and takes photos of them. I lean against a palm tree and watch how he goes about it, impressed by the portraits he shared with me last night.

An old woman works away, unbothered by us, in a shack on the other side of the path to the village. A man walks past with only a passing glance at the antics of Renato, this wild fifty-odd-year-old man with the energy and vibrancy of someone half his age. His oversized red shirt flaps around his gangly limbs as he moves, talking to and positioning the children in the place for the photo he sees. He talks in English but it doesn't matter – he is all tone and body language. Soon ten children flood onto the sand and Renato tries madly to isolate one or another from the throng.

I wander over and begin chatting to the children in Burmese. Propped on the bulbous base of a palm tree, I play question and answer, the kids finding my name, and my Burmese, hilarious.

'*Je naw nam-eh Le-o,*' I say to an uproar.

Rene makes a lion impression and I play along. The children all tell me their names, some shyer than others, the leader a bright boy of eleven who knows some English. We get onto ages, and the youngest, a two-year-old, answers with his fingers. The children are gorgeous – soft brown hair, cheeks crusted with *thanaka*, deep brown eyes, round, full faces and colourful clothes. They mill around and the eldest asks if I've eaten.

When we go to leave, the eldest boy asks for a drink of water and I realise with shame I have not responded to their hospitality in kind. The children joyfully pass the bottle around, spilling it on each other, such is their unvoiced thirst. Renato gives me another sound piece of advice – to buy some balloons for future occasions such as these.

On the far side of the village, a vast area of the beach is covered in straw and fishing nets. Women squat and advance from one foot to the other as they pick through the long nets for small fish. Full-bellied dogs leave the ones the women discard lying wide-eyed on the straw.

*

Stubble-cheeked after a week on the move, we stop at the barber. I grit my teeth as he uses no water, and not much of the cream from a rusty can of Gillette, until my face is smarting but smooth.

*

'*Kai-ta, kai-ta, kai-ta,*' say two little girls as they bob up and down in time.

'*Kai-ta, kai-ta,*' I say, holding my ears like they do as I bob up and down too.

They laugh and laugh, full of energy after a treat. Grandmother teases them from a chair in the corner.

I take a seat at one of the blue and white patterned tables deep in the restaurant and face the street.

'No onion, no onion,' says the waitress in Burmese when I walk in, poking fun at my effort to learn the phrase last night. Her grandmother gives her an instruction and I catch her pout and pretend to look scared. She laughs and carries trays of food outside past her father, who sits motionless in a dim corner with his phone. A shiny motorbike stands in the middle of the store in a gap between the tables.

The chef brings my meal out herself – she knows I like it. It is steaming hot and delicious, full of chilli and ginger. Each bowl aids my throat and energy and eases my fear that I've caught a mosquito-borne disease through carelessness.

The father suddenly rises, walks over the road and rides north on a scooter. The waitress tucks his chair in and I drink smoky green tea between spoons of soup. The mother of the family comes in on a scooter and we say hello to each other.

'Are you happy?'

'I am happy.' I say. 'Are you happy?'

'I am happy.'

I write the phrase in my notebook.

Three young men come in and order beers. They send the waitress back for cleaner glasses. She wipes the table and slaps one on the shoulder as they joke. The family sit at a wooden table on the end of a glass counter full of whiskey bottles. The little girls play in the corner, where the grandmother lights a fat rollie made with a single tobacco leaf.

*

I sit high above Ngapali on a hill between the main road and Ngapali dam. The reservoir is grey under the clouds and ripples in a light wind which carries spitting rain. Water lilies mass in the shallows next to an old bamboo raft. The sun breaks through the clouds, bright and brilliant, as I chat with four young women I passed on the dam wall.

The sun burns a flaming orange path from the horizon to the shore across the bold emerald sea. Fishing boats bob in the bay, shielded by a point of dense green growth. The group return and I remember passing tall gates to arrive. Worrying I'll be locked in, I hurry off. I take a photo of them before the sunset and ask them to email it to me. When I see the sky is burning to the northern horizon, I swing by the hostel to grab Renato and we hotfoot it to a secluded resort beach to watch the glowing embers of sky fade.

*

Renato and I take a few turns around the main street on the bikes and he teaches me how to say good evening in German. We greet those we suspect as wealthy Germanics in the street and receive the odd *'Guten abend'* in reply.

I continue to see the beauty. Lizards in the lamp posts, fish below the oil; a scabrous, hairless old dog fed rice outside the hair and betel juice-strewn ground of the barber's shop, a street dog carrying away an open coconut; the spoke pattern of crab hole refuse as they excavate sand; the ironic roar of muffled five-wheel carts as they pass the no-horn signs erected for swanky resorts despite the dark blind corners; the abused arm, bone-thin, of an older man passing in the fishing village, the schoolchildren chasing each other around the foul dam; the smell of alcohol on the bloodshot-eyed A-tho's breath the first night we met, which was such a deception; the fish jumping out of the polluted channel in Pathein. There is plentiful beauty amidst the foul in Myanmar. There is a lot of life here.

10

Linn Thar and Thandwe

Renato and I ride to Thandwe on old bicycles, passing huge walled military barracks and strings of new power poles waiting to stand next to the road. On the edge of Thandwe, we eat under a tin lean-to where pots full of fish and vegetables bubble and steam. At the market, we meet the woman from the drink stall where we stopped on the way to the fishing village. She is regal in a rich dress of pink and gold, has her hair pinned, and with purpose moves through the crowd. She helps me find a journal and then goes about her day's business. The market sprawls under blue tarpaulins, and the piles of fish covered in flies remind me of Gwa. People squeeze through narrow passageways and there is a relief in breaking free of the throng to the sunny main road. We sit on small wooden stools across the road, drinking iced coffee, taking a breather in the shade.

A woman in a tattered and faded pink top hauls load after load of water from a deep, dirty brick well with a bucket on a rope. Two more join her and they empty their buckets into big yellow jerrycans. In front of the coffee shop a woman makes ice cream and syrup milkshakes for boys and girls who sit and drink, spooning out berries. The women finish hauling water. The first hoists the heavy jerrycan onto her hip, picks up her smart phone from the well's lip and walks across the road and away.

We tie the bikes to the steel bars of a pick-up and I slide onto the long wooden bench seat as Renato stands on the back and we rattle home.

*

Fishermen wade out from the shore of the estuary next to the guest house, dragging a net between them. They slap the surface with palm fronds to stun the fish. Each slap raises long thin plumes of water as if the water has grown its own fronds. On the far bank, a pack of dogs roam through the reeds.

Three men work to repair the *Pinle Kyar Gyi*, a fishing boat lying on an angle in the mud of a mangrove at low tide. They hammer wooden dowels into each hole and saw off the ends. A generator thrums away and one man has a power sander hooked up to it via a series of extension leads. The boat is orange with white trimming and colourful silk flags hang in the rigging. The eldest man wears a green longyi and white singlet, the youngest a football jersey. The boat rests on hollow palm logs and rocks from side to side as they work. Mudskippers dart about in the shallows, their holes dotting the shore. Water drips out the bottom of the boat. The sander spits over the side. Resin patches and the dark stubs of old dowels dot the boat's flank from the many past days work on the thick wooden hull. The old man saws some dowels and hammers others, the thwump of the blows echoing from across the estuary. A fisherman's hut sits at the end of the wooden jetty, up on timber struts encased in collapsing brick piles. The corner hangs loose, its support keeled over in the mud. The youngest man eats out of a polystyrene box propped on the high side of the boat. A school of young fish the size of a finger stir up the shallow water, covered in a thin layer of oil. The three-day job is begun. The hull sits smooth, all its spines vanquished.

*

I open my journal and five children crowd around to see the words take shape. Two crouch on flat footballs and another squats next to me before sitting down. They chatter away at the sight before settling, returning to inspect the work between kicking around a football. We sit behind the heavy bamboo goalposts and a crowd of thirty or forty young men playing a furious full field match. They play shirts and skins and the bored goalkeepers at the near end take penalties and wait for the action to return. Plastic is strewn over the field unnoticed.

Past the pitch, cattle graze between haystacks. A hut with a roof of blue tin and palm leaves is in front of a stand of jungle with a cultivation of banana trees and palms. A little boy points a plastic gun at me. 'Bang!'

The children show off their Superman figurine with a red light on his chest. A farmer walks back and forth across the field with a cow and a dog and loses a cow each time. Others lead the cattle to shelter around the back of the goals.

The sky is thick with soft clouds and lightens in the west as the sun falls.

The boys laugh at the confusion on my face as I search for the essence of their lives. Three remain, speaking a steady stream, two in school uniform.

A man retires from the action covered in sweat. They park their scooters and motorbikes in a corner of the field near a new bamboo clubhouse. A woman collects hay from the field to keep the cattle overnight. Crows fly amongst the trees in the bright blue monastery which overlooks the field. A father with a jet-black pup feeds it from his hand with my companions fleeing to watch. I am part of the landscape now. The megaphones on the main street on the other side of the pagoda blare today's message.

The pup leaves and new company arrives. One reads a few words over my shoulder. I wait for the soft light of sunset to frame a photo.

The game is quick, the thin men racing around without an inch of fat to spare. They break for a minute, some sitting legs out, before going again. The first shot is re-energised, pounding into the crossbar and dislodging a T-shirt hung to dry.

A man across the fields takes the quick short steps of one with a heavy load, bearing a yoke hung with two yellow jerrycans full of water.

A Buddhist boy chops wood in the slopes of the monastery and looks out for a moment before gathering another armful.

11

Linn Thar to Taungup

One of the Frenchwomen hugs me goodbye and apologises for not spending time with us. At the restaurant I eat a last bowl of soup, ponder the nature of missed connections, give the waitress my drink bottle and thank them all for the nourishment.

I wait for the bus, anxious about it arriving on time, somewhere deeper of the next step without Renato. I head north to Mrauk-U, he south to Yangon, and for the third time in a week comes the pain of farewell. Clambering into the dark bus, I push aside the curtains and wave goodbye.

*

The bus depot overlooks a wide, shallow river where two men wade out with a net. Immense steel beams resting on concrete pillars bear a bridge to the distant side. The ripples from the men's movements travel up and down the surface. An egret flies away when I arrive. The near bank is planted with tomatoes, corn and rubbish. A group of children climb towards me. Two tourists stand on the bridge and the children gather round before moving on. The men leave the river with a catch of fish bunched in their net.

I squat in the yard of the bus depot, elbows resting on the insides of my knees in the local style, waiting for the next bus. Another young traveller approaches me full of eagerness to talk and question and know more about this country. I understand his eagerness in a place which raises so many questions, but the bus is leaving. We say goodbye and leave each other with our questions.

*

The refrigerated bus delivers its chilled cargo into a chaotic depot in Taungup. The crowd of passengers and taxi drivers is noisy, frantic and more than I can take, so I walk straight out of the depot and along the road. Feeling worn and grumpy, I don't care which way I go. A scooter driver who is in the same mood stops me along the road and takes me to buy a ticket for the boat to Sittwe then to find a room. The guest house offer me what they say is their only room, a big windowless one on the top floor, for a high price. When I walk away, they relent and give me one of the cheap local rooms, tiny and angular with a bed and a lock to see me through the night.

*

With an hour or so of light in the day, another one where distance and time have an unpredictable relationship, I walk out of town towards the hills. The road narrows as it climbs through tangled slopes before opening to the world and an old man washing by a well. Beyond him, Buddha stands twenty feet tall on the hilltop watching the sun set. He overlooks a valley filled with the sound of scooters, roosters and the growing animal chorus which welcomes the coming night. He has been freshly painted in gold and holds his robe between thumb and forefinger of his left hand, all four fingers pointing to the ground. A faded white and pink lotus flower supports his great weight, along with a golden ball and a branch by his feet. A monk crouches below me at the base of the pedestal. The monastery of two is a simple wooden house with a rusty tin roof. On a higher hill to the east is a pagoda the whole town can see. The second monk talks to the first, who stands in acquiescence.

The sun breaks through the clouds to illuminate Buddha, his robes becoming shadow and light. The two monks sit discussing my writing and the place. On a white pillar perches a golden rooster with a fine metalwork cone hanging from its beak. Lotus flowers open in four directions from above and below the pillar's gold bands. The sun shines orange, and colours the bottom of the clouds to pure mauve with orange-white skirts. The monks assume a cross-legged position, heads erect, eyes only for the distance and the sunset when I take a photo.

A stone statue with a broken arm and a protective dog sits cross legged on a hillock behind, facing due west. A monk from the stone pagoda's hillock hammers away at a bamboo shelter. The sun falls fast and the monks go inside to ready dinner.

*

A man who walked by as I left the *toya* returns on a scooter to give me a lift into town. I suppose the monks asked him to and hop on. We begin to ride past all the people I greeted and who greeted me on my walk to the *toya*, so when he stops to say hello to a friend I insist that I'm happy walking and continue on foot; past the monastery where I watched a group of monks perched on the roof of a building painting its beams, past a football field where I join in a game of *haki* with a rattan ball with a group who earlier were playing foot volley at the end of the village road, where it began to snake upwards into the jungle, where the air becomes cool and fresh after the choking dust of the main road, the group distinguishable by one who wears a loincloth, his bare buttocks a site unseen in my travels here, then past the store where I bought a drink, where I find the same nuts I bought in Yangon, past houses full of waving hands and smiling faces, before after a detour through the town's back streets I arrive at a junction to see the shining gold spine of the town pagoda, lit up with strong incandescent spotlights, which draw me in with as much power as they do the band of moths which dance in the dusty haze lifted by the passing traffic.

I sit cross-legged on the ground and a man sitting in a plastic chair offers me his, then brings me one from inside. I sit but feel more at ease cross-legged and return to the tiles. An older couple sit in front of the main shrine, with three statues within. The man is as a rock, motionless in an asymmetric lean to his left, as his wife sits tall and erect between frequent prostrations.

People come over wanting only to talk for a moment, watch me write, chat with me via one who speaks English and then amongst themselves in turns. They ask me for a photo and I return the favour shown me by the monks before they leave. My stiff and sore hips push me to dinner, and two of the boys from the second group ride me back to the guest house, where there is a restaurant on the second floor. I yelp over the bumps as I sit on the metal rack and the boys laugh.

*

In the upstairs restaurant, young men watch the television on the wall and talk little. The soup I order arrives full of all manner of seafood. I realise halfway through the bowl that the phrase for 'no meat' will only go so far. I eat the soup anyway and go to bed. In bed, I look out the window to the street and let the conversation of the men smoking outside float through the gap at the top of the wall and lull me to sleep.

12

Taungup to Sittwe

At five a.m., the scooter's passage through the cold air and drizzle to the docks clears my bleary eyes. In the light of a restaurant surrounded by darkness, I eat a fried egg and rice with a scalding cup of tea. Rain from the invisible sky lands on the palm thatch. Passing boats without lights generate a deep audible thrum on the pitch-black river. The boat is a large cruising ferry with cinema-like seats and I sit and talk with an Irishman before the motors roar into life and we slide away from the jetty.

*

At the bridge with the crew I watch the red and white roses on the prow lead the ferry north-west as the dawn light grows. Their shrine houses a statue of Buddha, a plastic lotus flower with a rainbow light and an offering of coconut scrolls and a thimble of water. The water ripples with a standing wave from the thrumming of the motors. I wander out the back to the surprise that the sun has already risen. It comes with the same lack of fanfare that it sets with over the Bay of Bengal, there one minute and gone the next. The risen sun continues its ascent up and behind a mass of cloud to begin a display of shade and colour, the dark grey and purple cloud releasing striped ribbons of orange and violet from its belly, while the top of its head shines bright white and its flanks a soft pale yellow, before the sun casts aside its shield and forges a shining path of gold to the rear of the boat, crinkling my brow and parting the once joined silhouette of land, tree and water through the revelation of colour. The mangroves shine a fresh, rich green over the murky emerald water after the rainfall.

The men at the stern welcome me with a hot coffee and a plastic chair to sit on. I perch out of their way and sip the coffee as the air rushes past the boat, driven by the roaring hum of the motors. Six wooden fishing boats fly by, tending nets between bamboo poles pointing out of the wrinkled sea at all angles. A lone boat, with a notch cut down the middle of its timber stern, heads into the rising sun as we head due north to Sittwe. The land moves like an old children's tin mobile with the front layer of mangroves sliding past a sluggish layer of hills. The sun winks at us from the gold pagodas marking villages dotted beyond the shore.

Swinging west, the boat passes a village among the mudflats. Its huts sit on tall stilts fixed in the mud and breathe clouds of white-grey smoke. The cool air smells of salt and fish. As the way narrows, the water ahead sits flat under the minute ripples of a light breeze. The boat's bow wave surges into the groves, breaking against trunk and bush. A canoe's pole mounted propeller breaks the water with a spray as it crosses the waves heading the other way. The boat pulls in to a small wooden jetty and the crew slow the heavy craft with sandals on outstretched feet. Men unload a heavy drum of fuel and a bulging white sack. The boat swings around, passing the emptiness of a new concrete jetty and an ancient stone pagoda on a hill.

On the glassy water, the mangroves rise and fall in the bow wave with an unreal smoothness, as if fixed to invisible uprights, and as the emerald water falls into the wave's trough, mudflats emerge, dark earthy brown against the bright mangrove leaves. Narrow channels offer glimpses of the winding depths of the river system. From next to a channel, a boy with skin the same colour as the earth he stands on watches the boat fly by. I glimpse him before the groves stretch shut to enclose their secrets. A man in a long wooden canoe lashes the motor in place and steers with a paddle.

At the edge of the sea and the groves, as we enter open water, an egret sits sentinel high atop a tree. Out to sea, the world fractures into layers of colour and movement again. On a point, dozens of egrets manage to fly while still, their forms like many pure white flags in the tree's canopy. The mangroves soar high into the air to make a dense green wall ten metres tall. The mobile gains a third layer as two canoes with shelters on their decks slide past. I stand in the sun and let it warm my back. Two seagulls take flight, one after the other, emptying their bowels and winging away.

We veer east into a narrow channel where crossed bamboo poles bar large craft from the offshoots. We veer again where the telltale rippling of the surface marks the meeting of two currents. The water becomes glass and flips the mangroves upside down, their green canopies separated by long black spider legs. Tall trees hint at solid ground but the pillars of a steel bridge which soars overhead run to the horizon.

A crocodile floats downriver and becomes a palm frond. The water is full of leaves and clouds before the wind comes and blows them all away. The twin motors sound a deep alternating bass beneath the constant whine. They sound like war drums, '*da-doon, doon, doon, da-doon, doon doon*'. With an explosion, the layers collide and hills erupt from the water's edge. A lonely red and orange canopy stands amongst a hundred different greens. In the east, on the mainland, humans mark hills with cleared slopes between the trees.

The layers split again, into near and far hills and sometimes hills neither near nor far. Power pylons dispute the virginity of the western hills. They are our bloody sheets on nature's balcony. We pass a tangled island. Its rocky beach and shadowy lee parody paradise. The sky's backing is static in this motion but different from moment to moment. Clouds return to blue water.

*

The island runs north–south and rises long and thin from the water like a serrated knife. Its shore is boulderous with few sandy beaches. It vanishes in the Bengali haze as we follow it north towards that distant corner of the world. The swell rocks the cabin and the back section is dark and full of diesel fumes. An industrial site comes into view, twelve immense tanks stood in place of an island, razed to the level of the sea. A haphazard shanty town contrasts with the immaculate and expansive site buildings. Now in open water there is only the boat and its people to see as the island is too distant to be anything but monotonous.

A sweat-soaked father comes above to wash his child who has soiled herself. He looks as distressed as his daughter but, for the noise or for fear of the water or for many an unknown reason, he doesn't take the crew's offer of a chair and returns to the boat's belly. A boy exits the door, hops onto the railing, leans down and closes the latch then spins his body up and over it to tend to a task. He wears a longyi and no life jacket.

We near the end of the knife and the beacon of a pagoda in the sun penetrates the haze. It sits two thirds of the way up a steep hill facing the water. In the sun in the back corner of the boat, earplugs in and foot vibrating on the lower rail, pages fight me in the wind. Over my left shoulder, where there was interminable sea and smog, another knife-like island parts the water.

*

From the jetty I convince the Irishman to share a scooter with me and we putter up the busy main road. The main tourist haunt is expensive but suits him so I continue on foot to find somewhere cheap to pass the night. I grow hotter and more tired in turns as I do a circuit of the area before settling on the Golden Guest House. The boat to Mrauk-U leaves tomorrow morning but buying a ticket is a challenge. The familiar smiles of locals disappear, replaced with scowling, impatient faces, and they try to fleece me for a phone call. The Burmese I learnt, slinging around a few phrases with abandon to get a laugh and a willing hand, is of a different dialect to that spoken here.

*

The city is a long way from its heyday and abandoned buildings dot the port side. The locals laugh when I ask if there is a beach, hoping to get a view of the sunset to salvage a moment of beauty from the place.

The Golden Guest House is a filthy place where, if lying on the bed I take off my glasses, I can imagine the white patches on the flaking blue wall are clouds, and the dirty mosquito net a wind-beaten sail on a yacht. Leaving my imaginings, I escape the guest house and wander north. I pass the Sittwe Tennis Club and wonder at the British whacking around tennis balls on a grass court long ago. Further on is a huge colonial building with tall pillars and a lawn. It is a tempting place to devour a boiled corn cob but the military feel from a government seal on the façade scares me off. A policeman stands in front of a fire-damaged mosque with a wall full of broken windows not far from the guest house. I find a restaurant and eat two meals of *tatalo-saa-me* to compensate for the atmosphere before returning to read of the jungle and dream of tomorrow.

13

Sittwe to Mrauk-U

At the Sittwe jetty, people huddle around a fire in the darkness, warming their hands, and I eat across the road with a monk sitting at the corner of my table. The meal is lukewarm, reheated from the day before and not as tasty as yesterday's. The woman of the restaurant jibes me on the way I say 'Thank you' and I am too jaded by all that is Sittwe to show her the generosity of good humour.

The slow boat is open to the elements with chairs set on the upper deck as if ready for a play. It is cold, and the two tourists I sit next to, one a man with a waxed moustache, are not much warmer. A young boy ferries an old lady across the river in a small canoe with a paddle, craft dot the banks and a man wades barefoot through the mud to untie the rope. I hawk up chesty muck and feel unwell. There is a flatness to many on board, an unchanging lowness of energy which I attribute to Sittwe itself.

We head east then north, the sun rising through a cool wind as we go. Fog covers the mudflats and trees smudge pastures split by small snaking rivers. A girl reaches into a plastic packet and tosses its treats into the air where seagulls break from the pursuing flock to snatch them in their beaks. When the packet is empty, she tosses it overboard too but the seagulls know better. It floats away in the wake.

The distant hilltops peeking out of an opaque mass show the fog is not the usual haze, which is fair in the way it obscures all things. Ramshackle villages line the banks and from the second floor of the boat cleared land is visible over a stand of mangroves.

The wind chills my ears and I wait for a narrowing of the river and for the sun to come out again to warm my bones. It hides behind a low-lying bank of cloud it found soon after clearing the horizon, yet when it emerges is still close enough to Earth's rim to shoot its rays far across the sky and spur colours from the clouds in a second sunrise.

Away from the banks, the fields are brown-stubbled and full of haystacks. I put my hand in my pocket and feel the mangrove fruit I plucked off a tree as it brushed against the boat at the second jetty yesterday. It ripens in my pocket and opens into six equal parts, protecting a green shoot entering a ball of fine, white threadlike roots. Outside a lonely house on the mud a small wind turbine spins in a blur. Higher clouds shade the sun again.

*

The river remains wide and the land flat in a huge expanse of delta. Long stilts attest to its breadth, lifting huts high above the mud for the time of flooding rains. Water buffalo take the place of cattle in the fields and stand still in the shallows like four-legged rocks.

At the prow of the boat on the upper deck, the moustached man sits drawing in the sun. I sit around the corner with my back to the steel bridge and the sun touches my chest through a thin jacket. A group of men on board strike up conversation as I sit on the prow writing. They crouch around me as I recite the funniest phrases I have. They joke about themselves and the big bearded American on board, one of them threatening to tweak up the leader's longyi to show the difference. The leader watches me keenly, rarely shifting his gaze to the delta. He carries a ten-thousand-kyat note in his breast pocket and we joke about who should buy the coffee. A young woman of eighteen sitting nearby travels with her parents. The men joke about me and her, saying she's very pretty. I give her the mangrove fruit.

The river has narrowed and the air is pleasant. Herds of buffalo are common and as we near Mrauk-U different pagodas, for a long time unsighted, appear. One looks Chinese, its many red-tiled roofs crowned in silver. A man paddles along in a canoe with no motor. The horn sounds as we round a tight bend and pairs of stone pagodas peek at us over the trees from far hilltops. Tour boats crowd the quays.

*

Steep hills surround the low-lying town and I pick my way up one of them as fast as my asthmatic lungs allow me to. A pagoda crowns the hill and a school boy sweeps its tiles and studies in turns. On a shaded wooden platform overlooking the town, I lie on my back, out of the hot sun and with a lulling distance to the town's noise, and sleep.

*

Down the hill, five female Buddhas surround a tree facing outwards. The base of the tree is coated in gold paint and the statues sit tall with thin waists and out-thrust bosoms. In the grounds of a temple, a bitch protects her pups with fierce barking before a passer-by calms her down.

The pile of timber offcuts and rolled-up palm matting lies on a tin-roofed shed's floor under the gaze of a dusty Buddha. His counterparts on either side have their eyes closed. The statues line a concrete plinth and wait to enter the temple whose foundations are being dug in the grounds. The shed hides behind two old brick pagodas, their moss-covered render worn and crumbling. A pile of prayer fans, shards of clay pottery, old cupboard doors and fluorescent tubes take up a corner. There is a collection of tarnished steel umbrellas from the pagoda towers. It is cool and shady out of the sun, with a tall stand of bamboo on the hill behind protecting the shed's roof. Red ants make a thick line of traffic on the staircase. The town's noise is distant and it feels as though few people come here. There is a vine-tangled red-brick pagoda north of the platform, the sun striking it and showing up the red and green colouring of its unrendered surface. The brick pagodas in front, although neglected, still have gold umbrellas atop. Behind

Buddha is some Burmese script on the wall; higher still, a few creepers make their tentative tentacled entrance.

*

Three women stand on a pile of jagged rocks striking them with sledgehammers. The steady, even ringing of the blows hits me before I see them. As I pass, one strikes a rock, sending a few chips flying but leaving it whole. I lower my head in shame and walk through the hot dust which puffs out from the heels of my sandals at every footfall. Not far up the road, a few children play in the grounds of a school, but are not in uniform or class. One, who says he is three but looks closer to five or six, speaks excellent English. I chat with them until the boy asks for money and my sense of innocence in the moment dissolves. I leave them with the inane advice to 'Be good', and continue up the road conscious of the ringing hammers of the women working behind me.

*

The temples show the fluctuations of modernity as each age brings a different style to the curved stone. Yet the differences of colour and shape and size hold the constancy of intention, an intention which gives the place a presence.

In front of an ancient walled temple, young men play *haki* and foot volley. The cattle gather for the night and a woman comes to collect her battery and solar panel. Goats graze the slopes of the fortress walls, which are in disrepair but with many metres of thickness to guard against the advances of time. Smoke haze from town hangs in the grassy depression. The well looks new, with a smooth concrete base, and people draw its water with jerrycans and tin urns. One man hauls a water drum up hand over hand and spills half on the ground when he empties it. The village creeps up its hill's slopes until thick bamboo eats it. The sun sinks from a cloudless sky behind the palms.

*

The villaged edge of town is a maze of curved dirt paths and hidden alleys and stairways full of curiosities. It is cooler, quieter and stalls sell bunches of small, thin-skinned bananas. The air is free of the choking dust of the town's streets. The banana skins rest in the bottom of the open drain. Children yell out whatever English they know and people I ask directions from are friendly and eager to help or to call out for someone who can. Ducks waddle across the road and the sweet voices of a man and woman singing in turn float from the centre of town. At an intersection, a policeman blockades the road and the sound of sirens grows. The sirens peak when a whistle-blowing man on a motorbike leads a cavalcade of vehicles through in a cloud of dust. Everyone stands and watches before the town's noise washes over the street and the dust settles. The sirens are not as loud as the singing Buddhists' megaphone.

*

The streets in Mrauk-U are narrow and the buildings remain open to the air. Through open doors and unshuttered windows is a view into a way of life which does not protect its privacy with the intensity of the culture I know. People sit watching television, two women kneel on a mat mending a blanket and talking, a man sits in a chair smoking. Soon after dark, the town retreats. The bamboo drying mats covered in tobacco leaves and spread out in the sun are rolled up, the main street stores close their concertina doors until only a few corner food vendors remain, and by eight o'clock the only crowd is a group of men and boys watching martial arts on a small mounted television in a bar. The side streets are very dark between the odd patch of light coming from a late-closing shop or a house which has power and the visible becomes invisible, a collection of indecipherable conversations coming from the dark, the smell of a cigar's smoke, the awareness of steady watching eyes which follow my passage towards the guest house.

14

Mrauk-U

Opposite the restaurant are two clothes stores open to the street and separated by a thin wall. On one side, a man with a white singlet stretched over his potbelly sits chewing betel. He rinses his mouth with a tin cup of water and a finger, while behind him, back to the wall facing the other way in the shop over, a teenager sits with her head still and strums her fingers on the arm of the chair. The man and the girl sit back to back for a long time, chewing and strumming and sitting in their shops.

The town moves and sounds and has its own rhythm, one where people pass the day in some way or another, whatever that way is. It is a school day, yet children work in shops or restaurants or float through the streets.

*

Over the bridge and up a dusty side road stands a vast rectangular gold gateway. Its thick square pillars stretch high into the air and the road winding through is small and humble with no bounding fences to mark its way. I pass through the great opening in search of the lake. Beyond it is a dry river bed, strewn with rubbish and grazed by ponies and kid goats. A village, a remnant of what stood before the dam emerged, perches on the steep slopes above the dry river bed. Following a thin but well worn trail along the riverbed is the valley's end. A tangled wall of hills rises on all sides, closing in as the valley narrows, before revealing two tombs, one old and one new. The path snakes on, up and then down into the next valley and an empty dam, now a soft grassy bowl shaded by huge trees. A monk works a small plot of ploughed land next to a hut and an ancient pagoda reduced to a crumbled mound of bricks. He lays grains of rice out to dry on a bamboo rack next to the path, which descends to the cool calm of a monastery. Angled sunlight and deep shadows create beautiful tapestries down its short passages. A cooking fire's smoke is thick and bright against the shadows, a passing monk's smooth scalp shines above his dark robes as if detached from the world.

I am soon noticed and meet the teacher who has lived here for seven years trailed by a group of children. I have reached the Aung-Menga-Lar Monastery. It is a sanctuary from the dust and heat of the bare land outside the valley and from the ceaseless noise of the town's streets. It is cool shadows and stone-edged pools of still water. It is a place of absolute peace. The teacher came here from Yangon. We talk a while before he assigns five guides to take me to the lake. The boys lead me there and return to the monastery, laughing as they run down the path back into the valley.

Beyond an old bluestone wall, atop a mound of earth damming the valley, sit hills of palms and pagodas. Their spires, bright gold against the black stone, shine back from the water, stirred by an imperceptible breeze. In the corner of the lake is a white-walled hut beside which half a dozen boys play foot volley. A huge old tree towers over the hut and next to its canopy, but some way behind on top of the highest hill in the area, is a young, completely gold pagoda. A thick archway splits the wall, its blocks of stone intact. Two monks walk past the arch from the hut, where they arrived by canoe. The four children who came up and watched me take a photo and write run through it yelling 'bye-bye' and waving.

Over the wall lies Mrauk-U, and smoke from the evening fires rises in thin clouds through the trees. A man in a bright red T-shirt paddles past, disappears, then returns into view going backwards and feeding his net out with his left hand. He puts the paddle on his lap and holds the net in his mouth for a moment.

A flock of birds fly across the saddle to the next lake, a valley across. A man on a bicycle rides to the foot of the path before halting and returning. The sound of hammering, or wood-chopping, carries over the water from a couple of huts on the far summit. The fisherman continues his slow drift across the water.

*

Two men from the village sit to talk with me, one an old teacher with excellent English. He talks of the troubles of the north of the Rakhine State, a place isolated from the rest of the country. He talks about the hard edges to the politics and vagaries of life in a poor place with an honesty and openness which strikes me, and is the answer to many of the questions borne since the morning, and since arriving in Sittwe. There is no work for him which is worth the pay as a teacher, so he tends his rice paddy instead. Little rain falls here, so he cultivates his paddy once a year. He says that in parts of Ayeyarwady, not far as the crow flies over the Arakan Yoma mountains, the paddies give three crops a year. Of a family of four or five children here, one or two might have the chance to go to school.

The conversation drifts towards politics when he says, 'If I try to fight the government for democracy, they will kill me.' The hardest edge of all keens in one sentence.

We sit and talk for a long time as we look over the lake with the sun easy in the late afternoon. The challenging nature of the conversation is set against the beauty of the place; the hardness of the past and the present is set against his warmth and friendliness and the depth of humanity so often found here.

*

I walk through the thick stone passage of the archway and follow the land as it drops into one of the villages. Long thoughts triggered by all that the man spoke about shift in my consciousness. Past one of the villages, I come to a strange gateway, grand and dark as it stands silhouetted against the twilight sky. My gaze drifts to the quarry next to it and I realise it's the same gateway I entered short hours ago. A strong pink sky forms above through the heavy layer of smoke hanging in the valley Mrauk-U occupies. From the main bridge, the river is a mirror. The dark objects floating in it are as indistinguishable as the pieces of rubbish they are as the clouds.

*

Wind chimes hang from the sagging door frames with doors concertinaed open to the street. The clothes stores are shut and the single-cylinder carts make a huge racket in the quiet evening. The owner is more animated as she sits in conversation with a friend. A Grand Royal Whiskey poster features Chelsea football club stars of yesteryear. A man covers his mouth as he works a toothpick as is the custom and I realise they smile with closed lips too.

15

Mrauk-U

I hole up in the same restaurant, watching life on the street. A man holds a red basket full of white bags in one hand and a child in a white hat with red dots on it in the other. A girl jogs after her friend's bike and hops on, sitting side-saddle. A middle-aged man bends his back against the handlebars of a trishaw loaded with heavy white sacks. He moves in slow motion through the dust as people flow around him like water around a snagged tree. Two boys with wild hairstyles walk by heading north, relaxed, the taller with his arm easily resting on the shoulder of the other, his hand dangling free. A woman with a sack of wood on her head walks by on the far side of the street and turns to look into a shop, the sack turning with her like a human weathervane. The noise drifts over me.

*

Three people pull up in an expensive black car, the first private car I've seen here, and enter the restaurant. The girls pull out chairs for them. The owner's son puts up a racket outside, throwing his bag around on his back as he waits to get picked up. The man who drove wears his hair in a bun and a big puffy jacket despite the heat. The lady wears a severe look and glass beads sewn onto her red dress. The young woman with her has thin-framed red glasses and a timid expression. A blue cardigan matches a rich and intricate dress of soft pinks and deep purples. They are not the first richly dressed people I've seen here.

A woman with a broken bicycle on her head passes with one hand up to steady it. The family's table fills with bowls of rice, meat and vegetables. The two girls serving watch their table closely. One fetches a palm fan which she waves to keep the flies away. The young woman takes it from her and puts it on her lap.

The ceiling fans sit caked in dust, still until the March heat comes. On the walls above the Grand Royal posters are three traditional works of powder and pebble. The middle is of a lady with an umbrella in a two-wheeled cart drawn by a sole brown Brahman cow. The cow in its gold trappings is goaded by a man in a wide palm hat. On the right, five women making music; the left, two women dancing, one arm up, one down, with elbows bent and palms facing outwards. The jacketed man looks at photos of the meal on his phone before starting the car to cool it down. The girls bring the bill. They leave and man holds the door open for the woman, returning my smile after a pause when we meet eyes.

A black goat sniffs its way along the edge of the market. A man holding a melon at head height in his backwards-facing palm crosses the street at an angle. On her left hip, an old woman carries a tin pot filled with corn. The girl from the store opposite sits as still in the same chair in bright colours. Two boys head south, the shorter with his hand on the shoulder of the taller. A man with an angry face and a hat with 'smart' on it in children's book lettering comes in to drink beer with two friends. The tangled wind chime on the left entrance twists ever so slowly on its nail.

*

A worn, jagged branch stands in the centre of a village dam marking the depth. Tall old trees and the stand of bamboo behind a monastery's wall shade the water. Washing lies on reeds and shrubs to dry in the bank's sun. Girls take water at the bottom of a worn path in the dam's corner closest to the village. Young boys shoot arrows from bamboo bows across the water as fish break the surface, soar into the air then return to their murky world. Near a stunted tree, the regrowth of an old stump, women beat clothes on rocks to clean them. A small solar panel propped against the tree finds power in the sun. The boys' arrows float in the dam. On the other side of one of the huts is a ruined pagoda, its central chamber open to the elements. In it sits a statue with no head; that of another, of a different shade, sits atop its broken neck.

A woman adjusts saffron longyis and sheets on a bamboo clothesline. A bare-chested man collects water in a tin urn. A bored boy follows the woman at the line, waiting for the top half of his robes to dry.

Two toddlers come and join the boys next to me after a cautious approach. One of the older boys copies what I say and does cartwheels along the bank. When I give him a balloon, he blows it up and the poor quality rubber bulges into a ridiculous shape that makes us laugh. The other boys toss clumps of dirt at him when he's at the water's edge and he thinks it's something in the water. I realise he might have a different ability as he turns to attack the bushes behind them with a piece of bamboo.

An old woman washes her hair sitting down, her husband bringing up water for her. One of the older boys grabs the toddler in green to put him in front of me; the toddler screams in distress and wails a while before running away. The one in orange soon follows, tackled by the teenager, and I tell the older boy to give him the balloon.

Far from the town's traffic, the chorus of the village rises in a constant buzzing of insects from grass and trees, the talking of the villagers, the sloshing of water from the dam, the barking of dogs and the wailing of a child. Birds call. Questions are asked and answered. A distant megaphone reaches us as the saffron garments disappear from the bamboo one by one.

The two toddlers are now three, all tiny and shy. They play at the base of the tree which shades the woman. Two women wring out a sopping sheet before one hangs it up, cracking it a couple of times to flatten its creases. A dead bamboo leaf falls and zigzags its way through the still air onto the water. A man grunts as he bends to dip two yellow jerries on a bamboo yoke into the dam. A little girl of no more than twelve carries the same load from the other corner.

*

The sun sets over Bangladesh. Light cloud overhead promises dusk beauty. Music plays on loudspeakers from the monastery below the hill where I sit with two stone pagodas. Mrauk-U carries on below. West of its hills and pagodas the land is dead flat, dotted with trees and the thin smudges of mangroves which mark the river's course. Far on the horizon is the dark bulk of a mountain range. Far behind, to the east, is another. A string of light globes on a wire joins the pagodas. Vines festoon their rusting gold umbrellas and one is set to topple. Three Buddhas watch the sun rise in the east, two dogs, crouching on their hind legs, guard them from the west. The hilltop is home to many colours; bright green and young red grass around the concrete base, pink and purple shoots with heads like lavender, tall bent bamboo with woody leaves ready to fall, white-ribbed stems with dandelion-like fluff, dark green shrubs and the old black pagodas. The tin roofs below come in many hues; rusty blood red next to shining red at the monastery, bright blue, clean grey tin and the up down pattern of red on grey where the corrugations rust. A halo of LEDs flickers through the monastery's open doorway. Bass thumps from someone's pickup on the main street. A scooter revs, a horn sounds, and the sun sinks below the mountain. Its orange light does not carry far and is soon a fingerprint on a big horizon.

Smoke again fills the valley as the eastern sky pinkens. The pagoda radiates the day's heat as I walk around it and speak my desires to the stones. 'Wisdom and clarity of thought, honesty and sincerity of word, kindness and compassion of action.'

Pink ribbons cut swaths of blue as the fading light touches thin bands of cloud. Sky blue fades to grey blue, melding with the smoke.

Starlings come out to hunt. Palm fronds rise above the smoke and hold their shape while distant trees blur then fade. The evening star, Venus, shines alone in the vault.

The horizon bulges in rich red-orange, before softening to pink and contracting. The mirrors of water become murky. The sun has set yet the sky holds onto its colour for longer than the land which is now all grey and black. Strings of lights shine on a nearby pagoda but not on these forgotten two. A far away fire on the plains is its only sign of people.

Music cranks from the monastery which is a hive of activity. The rock of Iron Cross in Metallica's style. On the other side of the hill Mrauk-U is as a mouse in comparison.

My stomach gurgles and my chin burns. I can barely see, yet still the horizon holds a dull pink glow. Stars come out and creatures creep through the undergrowth.

16

Mrauk-U

At a table in the restaurant I notice red words on my glass of green tea.

> Flower in the crannied wall
> I pluck you out of the crannies
> I hold you here, root and all, in my hand
> Little flower but if I could understand
> What you are, root and all, and all in all
> I should know what God and man is.
> Alfred Lord Tennyson

Another cosmic coincidence, as I try and hold myself, root and all, in my hand. Under the artworks of the women dancing, travelling and making music sit the three young waitresses. They sit without word or action, one facing the street, one the wall behind me and one the kitchen, their stillness in contrast to the movement of the art. The Chelsea players look dully across the room from their poster, unsurprised at finding themselves so far from England.

I frame a photo and put them in action. I sit and wait. The girls get up and a man comes and sits at one of the tables. The shot is gone. Another coffee whiles the time. The man leaves, two of the three sit down, then the green-jacketed lady from yesterday comes in. I give up my amateur photography and head out walking.

*

The stone palace walls are twenty feet tall and cool on my thighs in the shade of a byen tree which stands at the bottom of the main stairway.

The grounds are empty ruins, with a grid of brick foundations around neat square holes. The 'tink, tink, tink' of small hammers on stone comes from two men working to repair the massive wall. Inside, goats mow the lawn. Next to the tree, three men sit on a tarpaulin-covered platform next to their scooters waiting for a fare. White sheets hang to dry between a grove of banana trees in the land opposite. Its thin wire fence has collapsed in one section and is now a gate of wire rolled back onto a post. Four dogs lie like town lions on a pile of grey dirt; three golden-coated bitches and a huge gold and white coloured male with a streak of Saint Bernard blood.

A policeman in full dark green uniform and sandals rides down the paved road towards the centre. On the other half of the road, where it becomes a thin dirt track, two women stroll with umbrellas.

*

The long rectangular stone building is still, cool and quiet. Through the small archway at the entrance, I can see the sun-soaked garden which surrounds it. Along all three walls are raised stone plinths where dozens of stone Buddhas sit in a line. They are all painted solid gold except one in ungarnished stone. They vary from half a metre to a metre tall, some have open eyes, some closed, and the tilt of back and head changes a little this way or that along the lines. Two circular holes in the back wall allow a little light and fresh air to enter. A fluorescent tube fixed above the entrance only makes the light from the garden brighter. The garden is covered in grass apart from a few plants in square concrete boxes, some blooming with beautiful pink flowers against bright green leaves, the others spindly succulents on the verge of collapse.

Beyond the plants and brown grass is a bare tree, the ground's wall and a hazy blue sky. The goat which wandered in out of the heat for a scratch has not returned. The thin metal gates in the archway stand wide open, inviting visitors. A woman enters the passage, breaking the constant 'too-too-too-too' of a bird. She guides a group of tourists who traipse inside.

'I don't think I'm the Buddha you're here to see,' I say.

They don't speak English and trail out. I move back where I was sitting in front of the central Buddha on the back wall. The stone arches above are crumbling, the threat of rockfall one more hurdle in the meditator's path. The bird's cry begins again.

*

The world falls away from Shwe Daung Pagoda, bounded only by the wall of mountains not far to the east which isolate the north of Rakhine State. Foothills split the land between Mrauk-U and the mountains into long, flat-bottomed valleys, the valleys split again into a brown and yellow patchwork of fields. Blue-roofed clumps of buildings hint at industrial areas and a line of power poles head due south. The near slope of a hill has collapsed, leaving smooth red-brown rock in place of the dark green jungle. Behind me the sun, still with an hour of fire left for the day, raises a squint and a sweat. Near rivers, the patchwork becomes one of pale and dark greens of vegetable crops.

Small birds with long upright tail feathers and tiny crests fall from the treetops to lower limbs. Flowers clot a leafless tree vibrant red against the far hazy hills. A flock of birds hop from one flower to the next. The brilliant gold umbrella of the Sal-ya-men-aung Pagoda is visible, the larger stone one of the Ratana-men-aung hides. The Last Post sounds from the south, the trumpet carrying clear up the hill as the group playing foot volley on a dirt field stand stock still.

*

I face west, sitting in the shadow of the two gold dragons who guard the stairway to the pagoda, and take in the magnificence before me. I can see all of Mrauk-U, its noise of construction and traffic and yelling floating up with the harshness of proximity removed. I can see Haridaung Pagoda, where I slept on the first day, bright gold on the flat hilltop. I can see La-kywattaw Pagoda, the two stone spires where I watched last night's sunset. I can see the Latt-say-kan Gate, and the blue-roofed shrine beyond the lake where I sat two evenings ago. I can see the huts and houses of Mrauk-U dotted amongst the thick mass of trees, and the high palace walls where I sat this afternoon. I can see the sun slip over the mountains a fraction further south than the day before as each day its path becomes higher and the village dams become a fraction lower. I can see flocks of birds heading for the lakes.

I take a photo for the Americans who pestered me with their incessant chatter as the sun fell. In this way, one acquires merit. The last crescent of the waning moon appears. The far-off dusting of clouds turn a soft peach. A red-robed monk circles an earthy brown stone pagoda far below. The evening star joins the moon. The broken dragon's head I rest my foot on warms it as the breeze chills my toes. The lake, the pagodas and the town will soon fade from sight. I move to leave and the clear sky around the moon becomes a strong bright mauve. Light purple rays emanate from the horizon between blue shadows. The cloud on the left, a vivid pink. On the right of the sun's path, the horizon is a purple-yellow mass. Invisible mountain tops demarcate the rays. It is beauty.

17

Mrauk-U to Magway

The cumulative small frustrations of travel mount to see me start the day scowling. My only jacket's zip breaks in the wash and at the bus depot there are no buses. Chilly and grim, I wonder if I'm in the right place. I sit in the sun with a mediocre breakfast of reheated rice in my belly and a reassurance that the bus comes first from Sittwe. Calmness comes, and so it goes. A coffee tantalises me but, with no idea of how long until the bus stops, I practise self-discipline instead. Skinny truck drivers take a long time to repack and cover a load. Time crawls by.

*

The bus rumbles along the floor of the valley and time passes now with the easy watching which comes in the first hours of a long bus trip. It is the free seeing before the jolting and bumping and airlessness tire the body and mind beyond the limits of curiosity and wonder. We are travelling down the western edge of the spine of mountains which hide the vast interior from the state of Rakhine. Haystacks and huts huddled by intersecting dirt roads dot the rich farmland. At a food hall in Shwe Ou, I eat *tatalo-saa-me* again, the dark brown marinated vegetables chewy and bitter.

We reach the end of the valley and venture into the foothills of the range where it descends into the sea. The road rises and falls with the land, as we cross one great jungle-covered finger to follow the coast until the next one lifts the Earth and we climb again. We cross great rivers on long bridges which span their rippled sheets of water. The

Dalet River keeps the distance between the towns of Swate Chaung and Kazukaing and the mountains watch each other over the divide. We break to take breath from the thick dust churned up by the buses and trucks on the road ahead of us.

From Kazukaing, the road climbs and climbs, the endless stretches of jungle and interminable twisting and turning of the bus snaking its way further east hypnotising, putting me in a trance-like state of thoughtless seeing. Signs for the China–Myanmar Gas Pipeline Project are staked to the odd corner and the tangled jungle yields to uniform stands of bamboo. Near the state border, roadside shanties of dust-coated tarpaulins and bamboo beams shelter families in the depths of poverty.

After eight hours of hard travelling, the sunset penetrates my mental fog as a stark horizontal line splits the world in two far to the west. It is a line between light and dark, touched and untouched, now and then. I gaze at the fading brilliance of the colourful haze above the blackness until there is no more a separation and everything outside the bus disappears.

At another roadhouse, I stretch my legs, fling a chewed corn cob into the jungle and piss in the water trough of a fetid toilet block by mistake, ignorant of the customs and repelled by the ankle-deep morass of water and urine in the centre of the concrete slab. I wish I watered a tree instead.

Later at night in the pitch darkness, the curves and bends end and we fly along a straight road. It is too late a relief for a body rag-dolled for over twelve hours.

The road to Bagan is on a different bus and at midnight the doors open to a deserted street on the outskirts of Magway, where I am assured there is a connection. The bus takes off in a blast of diesel and dust. I stand with my pack and a group of scooter drivers to find that there is no bus departing from this lonely corner. I seethe with the quick anger which comes with a sense of tired vulnerability.

*

After a ride to the depot on the back of a scooter, I find that there is no connecting bus until the morning. While I walk around the depot searching in vain for a connecting service, I meet a man who offers me a place to sleep for only five thousand kyat and a ride on a bus at seven a.m. In my stubbornness, I ask him to wait as I do a full lap of the depot to confirm there is no other option.

When I return, he is gone, and the men sitting in the foyer of the ticket office he had pointed me to say, 'No, you can't sleep here.'

I am low on cash and desperate for a safe place to sleep. I wander the depot and meet a young man, who says '*Ho-te*' when I ask him where I can sleep.

'No expensive, I need cheap,' I say in Burmese, and he says, 'Sleeping, van,' pointing to the people mover next to him.

I lie on my back in the middle row, legs tucked up, and from there ponder the wisdom of my choice. We are in a boom-gated, guarded compound, I will wake if the van starts, my cash and passport are in my shirt and it's Myanmar. I decide it's safe with joy. The van smells of sweat, betel and the liquor on the breath of one of the three men asleep in the van who leans over the back row of seats to greet me. I am covered with sweat – the old of the day's travel and the new of the last hour's stresses – and find sleep elusive.

In the small hours, I wake with the cold, crawl into my sleeping bag and wake again when a man yells and bangs on the van's windows. As the others do, I lie dead still and silent until he goes away.

18

Magway to Nyaung-U

When morning arrives, I am so cosy that only the coming departure of the bus gets me up. I give the man who invited me to share the van a few thousand kyat, buy a ticket to Nyaung-U and in the cool early light wander outside the depot. Sleep rims my eyes as I walk around the block looking at the food stalls.

I hop into the van for an easy three-hour trip to Nyaung-U, the township before Bagan. We cross the inland plain of red earth and dry scratchy trees. It is a world away from the rich coastal valleys and lush jungle-carpeted mountains. A good tip from Renato sees me in my first dorm room of the trip by midday. My energy flags, but I hire a bicycle and ride through the hot dusty streets. It feels good to move under my own power and enliven the blood in my heavy limbs.

Not far from the township is a large temple with a long roofed market leading into it from the road. I park my bike and walk through the cool passage, chatting with a stall holder before buying a copy of *Burmese Days*. The central pagoda has a roof of red tin with a faded layer of gold paint which imparts a tone of mottled provinciality to the temple. It fits the unkempt grounds, cracked concrete and crude cyclone wire fences which keep people at arms reach from the statues within. A woman sleeps soundly on the marble with her head resting on a brick. The white stone is hot in the sun and cool in the shade under my bare feet. I walk here and there with no intentions and run into difficulty when two women offer me a flower to give to the deities for a blessing. I have the flower in my hand before realising this blessing costs, and give the flower back to them without one. I sit on the marble near the sleeping woman to write for a while and catch my thoughts after a full day of movement.

On a square wooden platform under a shady tree in a quiet corner of the pagoda's large grounds, I fall asleep. A few dogs scrap in a corner, a cat cleans itself between two statues of a shrine girt tree, dirt and trees fill the area beyond the central square. Nuts dislodged by birds above drop to the ground. A tap behind a tin-roofed squat toilet drip, drip, drips, splashing the wall's growth of green slime. Bells ring out.

I come in and out of consciousness to see the sky parted by the gentle movement of leaves in the tree above me. When I wake fully, I am rejuvenated. There are tourists everywhere who I'm looking forward to meeting, and I've got a bike and a set of lungs fit enough to explore with.

*

The bike creaks with me down long flat roads. An effort to reconcile their twists with the map I picked up at the hostel is futile, then I go free, riding along. A long strip of palms split the main road from Nyaung-U to Old Bagan. Not far outside Nyaung-U, timeless red clay pagodas rise from the earth. Some are inconspicuous, hidden by trees, others soar into the sky from the tops of vast walled temples. As the sun grows weary of the day, the way becomes busier as half the tourist population of Myanmar hare through dusty back roads. They are in search of the perfect spot from which to watch the sun catch Earth's distant rim. Some go by bike, others by car, some in coaches which lurch along the rutted roads and some in two-wheeled wagons led by Brahman cattle. I marvel at the rush of desire and drink the excitement of the chase, meeting two couples on bike who I follow with the freedom of having no destination. The dust tossed up by the passage of many people becomes pure gold in the light, the people moving through it are jet-black silhouettes, sinuous and stark ahead of me.

We find a temple where we can scramble to the roof and climb dark stairwells to meet a soft sunset and the expanse of the pagoda-dotted plain. Most tourists leave with the sun, and minutes from the swarming crowd we enjoy the absurdity of having the roof to ourselves. We watch the stars come out and feel the air cool on our limbs. We imagine camping out for the night. We talk of our travels, of chance encounters, and set a time for a reunion later in the night when I go my way and they, theirs.

*

At the hostel, I meet happy tourists, chat with a warm Frenchwoman and take off to find a meal and a bottle of beer to take to my sunset friends. Away from the smoke and dust trapped in Mrauk-U's valley and invigorated by the wonder of the plains, I am stronger by the hour. I pedal smoothly on the bike, looking around as I go, before a flash of recognition comes with meeting the eyes of a lady outside a local restaurant. A moment later, I swing the bike around and pull up at her table. She sits alone with a denim shirt and bright eyes and the softest face in a country of soft faces. I sit down opposite and see she is someone I've never seen before. She talks and I question, and she talks until she talks and I listen, and she talks. We arrange to meet in the morning and I ride into the cool darkness of the gentle downwards slope to Bagan, happy.

At my sunset friends' hotel, we drink and talk late into the night. Myanmar excites us. Travelling excites us. Living with a warmth of feeling and an easy appreciation of the world excites us.

19

Nyaung-U and Bagan

Amanda arrives as I sit in the sun on the blue-tiled patio of the hostel. The morning is bright and clear. We find out if we can share a room at the Pyensa Rupa Guest House up the street. The man who looks after the guest house oozes cool calmness. He has lush black 1970s rocker hair and a big smile. The room is airy, two beds, light pink tiles, a window to the outside world and a big bathroom. I drop off my backpack and we take off on an electric scooter from the store next door. Her presence behind me is welcome and exciting.

After ambling around the dusty roads near where last night's sun set, we perch on the wall of a modest temple, look over the plain and she tells me of her life. I listen intently as I immerse myself in the incredible scene of pagodas and palms stretching into the distance. We brush against each other in a dance careful and careless in turns, taking a hand here, touching an elbow there, rubbing shoulders and meeting eyes. For a while, we know each other in stillness, then move again.

Outside a big temple, a small market droops in the heat. Bells ring out. They hang in bands from a small stall and jostle each other in the wind. A collection of sandals stand in pairs at the cool stone entrance to an ancient, towering pagoda. A man stands holding a cotton parasol and waiting for the right price. Buddha's stone incarnations sit in dim passageways trodden by tourists but not monks. At the back of the temple is a huge stone room open to the air. There a man crouches, concentrating on his work, applying grained paint to sheets of cloth. Fantastic designs of dragons, elephants, Buddha and the imagery of a nation many times divided and reunited jump from the cloth.

We explore the nooks and crannies, cool passages and pitch-black staircases which lead onto sunlit roofs in blinding bursts of light. A huge statue metres tall and locked in a temple surprises us. Brick kilns fuelled by palm stems huff black smoke, huts hide from the main road along narrow dirt tracks and a crying girl stands with her arms tied to a tree. Our guts knot and we stop, then go, in heavy talk of the rightness of action or inaction across cultures.

In the distance of the plain we see a many-storeyed tower but cannot find our way to its base along the winding tracks. It comes closer and closer then the track bends and we go further and further away. The track we follow leads to the village of Minnanthu, where a bright young girl halts us with her offer of dinner and a tour of the town in flawless English. We feast while the girl tries her hand at matchmaking. While there is light, we wander to the other side of town to sit above the football field and watch the sun set. There is a crisp whiteness to the painted temples which grows with the blueing light.

Promising to return and see the village tomorrow, we set off for the guest house in the dark, the scooter's battery ailing. I drive past offers of help before the reality of distance and darkness hits and strands us on a highway corner. A group of men in a taxi pull over when we wave. They lock up the scooter, arrange its collection, drive us home and wish us only the best.

A shower eases my frazzled state before we unwind the activity of the day and wander up the street for dinner. Amanda buys a small bottle of rum and we eat and drink and talk in the airy restaurant next to the street. It is cool and shadowed and has lost its dusty daylight haste.

In the room we found in the morning, a full day ago, we sit cross-legged on her bed talking, laughing and being until the moment when words become meaningless, I lean towards her, and we kiss a day's anticipation away.

20

Nyaung-U

Four locals sit in low plastic easy chairs opposite us in the tea house. An older man dressed like a tree in a dark green longyi and light green polo sits with his knee up and his hand wrapped around the back of his head watching the TV on the wall. A pack of cigarettes bulge in his breast pocket. A young man with a Justin Bieber T-shirt leans over him and wraps his arms around his neck, singing and checking his phone. The three others at the table sit with faces as impassive as those of stone statues. One twirls his keys, the other plays music videos on a tablet and the third, face plastered with *thanaka*, smokes.

*

The road to the village is smooth and we cruise along, pass the place where we gave up the scooter last night, and turn onto the dirt track. The young girl is outside the restaurant with her big smile and happy to show us her village. Brahman cattle feed under a bamboo shelter, and when working walk in small circles around a stone mill. Rooms are filled with bright lacquer ware and handmade cloth. In a brick-floored hut, a lady with bright, clear eyes and a face of many deep lines makes cheroots. She deftly slices thin chips from a dried palm stem into a bowl, separates yellow corn husks and fills them with a mixture of tobacco, herbs and palm chips. Her cheroot smoulders in a wooden bowl. She finishes crafting the cheroot, adds it to the pile by her side then takes hers, sparks it up, sits back on her heels and surrounds herself with thick fragrant smoke.

*

As the sun puts on its afternoon coat of gold, we go to the tower and its restaurant far above the plain. Amanda is afraid of heights and grips the stair's banister with one hand and my arm with the other. She looks into the distance while I look at the diminished buildings nine floors below. A crowd of tourists lugging the best cameras money can buy document the sun's journey home. We eat and talk and laugh with the waiter, who is as unused to our manners as we are to his, before returning through the darkness with warm bellies and no scooter woes.

Our evening of luxury begs a finishing touch. We lie on our backs in the family home of a lovely round Burmese lady. With her friend, she pats, pinches and rubs our chests, legs then backs in the traditional style while Amanda and I giggle. They chat in Burmese, a young girl laughs at cartoons on the TV in the corner and a young man comes and goes teasing her. He emanates a sense of easy style, his hair tied back and a relaxed smile playing on his face.

Late at night, we sit on the roof of the guest house smoking a cheroot from the village. After a few puffs, we float away, a little dizzy and a little lighter, before leaving half in a bowl for tomorrow. The cheroot maker smokes three a day.

21

Mount Popa

At the foot of Mount Popa stands a fifteen-foot tall man holding a flag in his upraised hand and scowling over the town. His narrow gaze is stern and his creased lips are set in the deep furrowed arcs of his cheeks from his nostrils. Thick Buddha-like eyebrows take a curling, curving path. A string of LEDs hang off his left shoulder and he rests two fingers on a pedestal-mounted globe of the world in shining gold. Flowers embroider the thick maroon robe. A brown cloth bag hangs around his neck on long draws so people level with his knees can put thousand-kyat notes inside. US dollars and kyat notes pinned to the bag flutter in the breeze. Mosaic mirrors stuck to the pale teal concrete decorate the three walls. Below the crude intrusion of a broken electrical wire is a pile of wooden stools and dishes. A round table and stool sit before his feet next to a set of crooked palm mats on wooden pallets. Over his silver-stranded hair is a fine tin umbrella and a naked light globe. A monkey sits in the corner eating nuts out of cones of newspaper and the noise of the school below comes clear up the hill. Rows of plaques dedicated to his donors break the mosaic with their unpainted grey grout. The plaques march on the mirrored tiling up the pillars and along the walls.

Young Burmese men come and spit over the low concrete wall before checking their appearance on smart phones and going. Metal gongs hang on thin rope off a bamboo pole held by a steel hook. People troop up and down the main staircase to the side. An orange red, green, and yellow banded flag moves limply on its pole as the tin roof shudders and shakes as monkeys chase each other around. A small one walks along with a blue stuffed toy in its mouth. Flowers wilt on top of the globe. A local woman climbs the stairs, puts a note in the bag, and leaves. The man's expression doesn't change.

*

Lines of leafy trees arch to form a shadowed tunnel framing the pagoda crowned Mount Popa. The immense rock shoots from the flat plain like a giant molar, complete with the gold cap of five pagodas and their accoutrements. Beyond the rock the dry, hot plains of central Myanmar fade into obscurity. The steep slopes glitter like the pagodas in the sun which bounces off the litter of plastic. Scanty trees and buildings cling to the cliffs and from a distance the glimmer is slow and still. There is no sign of the inner chaos where small monkeys run wild among the thong of Burmese and Chinese tourists. They leap off with easy pickings of water bottles, food and toys.

At each pagoda's shrine, men call in monotonous strings of Burmese for donations. Kyat notes spill from gold statues, pinned to their robes and stuffed into glass boxes at their feet. Groups of Chinese tourists form long, close lines on the stairs, plodding up one foot then the next. On the open summit they wear long shirts, gloves, hats and sunglasses against the sun but are defenceless against the monkeys. They stay close in a defensive huddle. At the wider entry flights, women sit and sell soft drinks, food and every possible piece of memorabilia.

Along the stairways the trail of smeared monkey dung and urine is broken for a few steps by a man with a mop and a wad of cash in one hand calling for tips. His call is the only English spoken on the mountain. The stairs going up are far cleaner than those going down as the pilgrims exhaust either their generosity or their desire for clean feet. The tiles on the stairs are chipped and cracked. Small balconies around the pagodas are full of building waste and rubble. Razor wire covers a satellite dish to block the monkeys who daintily hop over it.

Across the plain at the Popa Mountain Resort, tranquillity and beauty reign. Birds sing from the trees. The top of the mountain has become a miraculous garden of shade and soft light, of cool bluestone paths beneath tall trees and a lush undergrowth of reeds and succulents. Polite staff farewell guests who eat from a rich buffet while overlooking the rock. The view over the greenery is unbroken as it stretches to the plains. The dry and dusty shrubs emblematic of those flat stretches fall from the lower reaches of the mountain. The horizon is smudged into the sky where thicker smoke lightens the darker dusty blue of the land into the same blue-white, a perfect canvas.

Leaves and butterflies drift from the canopy as a couple staying in a villa next to the path discuss plans for the afternoon: tea or coffee, or Scotch?

22

Nyaung-U

Amanda arranges her hair and looks at the artist who transports her form onto glossy paper. She has an oval face with upturned lips and curly brunette hair which falls in rings over her shoulders. Her tawny eyes are framed by the arches of Persian eyebrows. Her lipstick is a pale salmon tint, light against her olive skin. She is wearing a bright orange button-up blouse with a string of small pearls around her neck and keeps her soft self-conscious smile as both the artist and I scratch away.

She says thank you in Burmese as the artist says, 'Your hair is so beautiful, like a poem.' He works fast; after sketching her face he stands and, bent over the table with one foot forward and one foot back, he attacks her hair. He has thin arms and legs and moves with the short, sharp precision of a bird.

She sits still with a smile playing on her face as the faces on the studio wall look on. Her eyes are bright as he finishes and she looks at the sketch, ready for colour. Her white teeth flash as she laughs at his compliments.

'Your hair, your eyes, your lips, very beautiful. The light in you comes out,' he says, spreading his arms outwards and lifting them upwards, 'for both of you.'

*

On the banks of the Ayeyarwady River, men perch on low wooden stools and play *bi-li* on a smooth wooden table. With a flick, they send a puck rocketing over the surface to knock tokens into the holes in the corner. The men have hands full of cards and eyes on the action, chatting all the while. Around the table, a crowd sit and stand, smoking and commenting. One man lies on his side on a bamboo bench with a thin moustache and a quizzical face. On the river, boats chug into the jetty, nearby small horses stand in the sun fidgeting and quivering at the flies. Their tails flick against tail bags of concrete sacks and the dusty canopies of the two wheel carts shake with them. Money changes hands and a player grumbles.

A fleet of vans and taxis crowd the riverbank waiting for the next ferry's arrival from Mandalay. A small patch of dirt is cultivated to grow gourds on a bamboo trellis and a few tourists wander around this curious dead end. Big dusty trees shade the shallow U of tea-shops, restaurants and stores. The Ayeyarwady is flat and steely under the late afternoon sun. A man thick with jackets crouches next to a pile of rubbish and picks through it. He finds a plastic bag of old rice and walks away in shorts and socks.

A ferry arrives and the game breaks up, the players settling their debts and going to wait for fares. They slap on the back of the head a man reluctant to leave, and laugh as he sits immobile before finally getting up. I sit down and play two rounds, losing one alone and winning with a partner but without the pitfalls of cards or cash. An impatient pro sits down in my place and destroys them, the game over in minutes.

Two girls come back from their washing with their wet hair slicked back on their heads and laugh when they see me looking at them from the bamboo bench. A man with an even dollop of paste on his toothbrush and a comb in a plastic basket wanders down to the water. A little boy of two or three hands me a copy of *Burmese Days* in French. I say I speak English, so he hands me *Twilight Over Burma* and after a short bargain I have a new book to read.

A beautiful, calm and warm energy comes over me during the walk to the guest house. The light of the setting sun through trees and alleys turns the dust into gold. It reminds me of the Brazilian riding his bicycle to the sunset on the first day in Bagan, a moving black silhouette on a sea of gold. I walk along with a light step and take the cool, quiet back streets, wading through a gentle river of hellos, smiles and greetings.

*

Amanda has a shower and packs her belongings before catching the bus to Yangon. We sit together in the foyer of the guest house waiting for the pickup to arrive to take her to the depot, making small talk, chatting with the man who looks after Pyensa Rupa and passing the uncomfortable moments before a farewell.

We say goodbye, hastily kissing as she piles into the back of the truck, and tears prick my eyes as I walk back into the guest house foyer where the man sits smoking his cigar. I head upstairs for a hot shower after first lying flat on my back in the pain. And so it goes.

'You'll be in my book,' Amanda said.

'And you'll be in mine.'

23

Nyaung-U to Nyaungshwe

The sky loses its heavy blackness as we ride along dirt tracks in a hurry to find the promised temple where we can watch the sun rise over Bagan. We drop our bikes next to the road and walk across indistinct furrows towards a group of pagodas in a field. The sky to the east parts into layers of pale ruby above and clay orange below. We emerge on the roof to see the dark spires surrounding us. Fog hangs heavy on the ground, hiding small temples and drawing the largest ones into prominence. The air is cool and still. Light grows adding colour to the red bricks amidst the green palms and brown earth fields. The dark strong hues of the eastern horizon fade into a pale glow as, above, the sky becomes a clear blue.

All of a sudden, strange curved shapes appear over the southern treetops, first in green, then gold and dark red. They wobble over the trees and swell with every minute, as if the palms have taken on a fantastic new form of life. They grow with the light and soon tower over the trees. When the sun first peeks over the far mountains, one detaches from the ground and floats upward like a ball of wax in a lava lamp. One by one, the magical beings lose their tethers, some seeking the sky with more eagerness than others. They rise with the sun and by the time it has cleared the mountains, only one is stuck fast beyond the trees.

The rising sun brings a new colour as the red bricks and green treetops become richer in their contrast. Pagodas shrouded in shadows or fog emerge, small and tucked between stands of trees. A farmer drives his cart to the field below us. As sunrise breaks the day, he breaks the soil with a wooden plough and two white Brahman bullocks.

The balloons drift with majesty across the sky and in a cosmic chance Luca and Leika from the guest house pass right over us. Jeffrey recognises them, yells hello and they yell and wave back. We stand on the roof of the temple waving and feeling small as they lean from the basket underneath their huge balloon to take a photograph.

*

We linger on the pagoda's roof as the sun warms us through, then return to the guest house for breakfast. Luca and Leika arrive and show us the photos they took from the balloon, brimming with excitement. We take off to meet Aline and Eliane and pull up in the car park of their hotel with a skid as we horse around on the scooters. They choose bicycles so we cruise around the tracks closer to Old Bagan, visiting more temples, markets and ancient wonders. We eat lunch high on the steep eastern bank of the river. The ladies go home for a swim and Jeffrey and I head further afield while we have the chance. On top of a huge square temple, one of the most distant of the thousands in the area, we look for long minutes over the vast heated plain which appears as the clay oven of a giant sculptor specialising in spiritual architecture.

*

After a refreshing dive into the pool of their classy resort, we sit in the sun and share of ourselves with a wonderful openness and enthusiasm. They are overwhelmingly enthusiastic, encouraging and appreciative.

Eliane shares her music; her voice is one of beauty. She plays a Kasey Chambers cover she recorded with a cold and tries to deflect our praise, then an original. Jeffrey is most appreciative of all and shares incredible photos of his travels in Cambodia and Laos. His creative pursuit comes through brilliant backdrops and sunsets. I linger with them by the pool until the time to leave comes. I say goodbye, and return to pack my things with the same aura as the evening before.

*

In the shower, I hear a knock on the door, and Leah, who is sharing the room with Jeffrey tonight, yells that the pickup has arrived, at six-fifteen not seven. I jump out of the shower, rush to dry and dress and am conscious not to forget my passport and cash. It is another hasty goodbye to the man from Pyensa Rupa, who has made a great impression upon me. I jump in the tray and apologise to the waiting pickup full of tourists. English and Spanish voices make chatter. We take off and make the depot in time. On the big bus, I meet Hiro, an energetic and talkative Japanese man. He has visited an incredible list of countries in the past six months, and has lost no passion for being on the move. Only my cough limits our conversation as the full day catches up with me.

At three a.m. and with only a few hours of poor sleep, we find a good man at Nyaungshwe who taxis us to the Primrose Hotel. It has cheap double rooms in a calm and still area of town. He makes sure we are looked after and insists we should not have to pay for the night as it's already half gone. I go to sleep with a great optimism, positivity and joy in life, travel and human connection after a wonderful day shared with Jeffrey and his friends, then Hiro. If there is no blind luck, then fortune is kind, for I was a few minutes away from missing the bus. It is a day which only gives from one morning to the next.

24

Nyaungshwe, Inle Lake

Hiro and I wake slowly and wander down to the canal. Long narrow boats motor by shops and restaurants stretching from the land on long stilts. We eat, hire bicycles and head west over a stone bridge and out of town along the northern reaches of Inle Lake.

On a hill overlooking the lake, high among the red dirt and the scrub, sit two buildings with rusting tin roofs. They face two pagodas, gold spires and white bases brilliant against the faded, dusty bush. The pagoda dotted slopes over the flat blue and brown expanse of water mirror the site. Two bamboo poles fly the frayed purple, red, white and pink flags of Buddhism. A steady breeze draws them tight, swaying the poles. Deciduous trees stand leafless in the winter heat, their branches thin and grey. The light and dark leaves of evergreens flutter on stilled trunks.

The near pagoda is built on top of a white cube with a slim miniature spire at each corner. Rectangular gilded openings extrude from the base walls, sheltering cross-legged Buddhas who face the world. A power cable stretches to a skew-whiff spotlight pointing at the ground.

An old woman lives here. She wanders up the path and the dogs set off another racket when I call out. She understands none of what I say. Unconcerned, she returns, perhaps to see where Hiro is.

The pagoda's face to the lake opens to a cool passage and a statue who has even here a halo of white lights set on gold tin. Expired offerings rest on a wooden and steel frame. Flowers stand in stale water next to red cotton umbrellas. Blackened wicks lie in the creamy white puddles of exhausted candles. The far pagoda is on the summit of a smaller hill below. It is taller and has another spire at each corner but is faded and weather-beaten. The monsoon's dirt streaks its walls and the crowning pagoda's golden coat shows white underneath. A cat meows as people ring the old bell at the lower pagoda, its tone beautiful and clear.

I sweep aside creepers and leaves to sit clear of the detritus on sharp rocks. Ants with black legs and mustard-tinted hairy bodies discover the mess of their road. They make me nervous as they scurry around their human detour. One crawls onto my foot but I resist the urge to slap it away and instead place my foot on the rock until it leaves. The unexpected danger is the tiny black ant, which I see when I am bitten has swarmed onto my leg. I stand and write.

Behind the house are concrete wells with tin covers held down by rocks and terracotta pots. An empty bamboo clothesline hangs between tree branches and poles. Far below on the lake shore is a village too small to merit a name on the map, a collection of red and grey tin broken by the blue of shining glass and new roofs between faded timber walls. The houses stand like herons on long straight legs. Old walnut trees surround me. Their leaves fade from bright red with green undersides, the last survivors as their companions coat the ground around in a carpet of light brown. Ragged black holes dot the carpet where caterpillars feasted before the leaves fell. The walnut trunks are gnarled and caked with red dust. Above them, the moon hangs in a light blue sky. A long thin streak of cirrus sits above the far hills.

Roosters and dogs talk in the village and from the lake floats a constant but light chugging of dozens of boats moving cargo and people. Their rotors raise high white sprays of water from where they sit below the surface. A long line of six boats take the same course along the shore. The lake wears the boats' paths like the slime of snails on a rock. The breeze pushes the straight lines out of kilter into organic weaves and curves. Far across the lake, a temple and a grassy island break through the depths. Monsoonal rain rounds and smooths the eastern hills coloured by pale red dirt where the trees are thin. Scattered buildings cling to the shoreline. Only a few pagodas venture higher up the slopes.

Overhead, birds loop and arc in easy thermals. The wind drops the flags before returning to clutter and scratch stiff leaves against the bare branches. A high hill to the west plucks the sting from the nearing sun. I smile.

*

Hiro and I ride ten kilometres back to Nyaungshwe as the last light draws away over the fields. It slides across the lake and up the distant slopes, which become a rich golden pink. We ride past fields of sugar cane, silvery heads twelve feet high, and stubble burning black and throwing up choking smoke. Tilled fields lie ready for sowing. Some farmers use the cow, some the buffalo, others a single-cylinder engine on steel tracks. The machine sits on top of the rice paddies' mud as the farmer wallows behind. As the northern sky takes on a vast haze of fading yellow and purple, which conjures all the majesty of a big sky over a big land, we turn onto the main east–west road into town and see a farmer chasing the last reluctant ducks into a wooden pen with a bamboo stick. Water buffalo settle down on the edge of the ditch between the road and the fields and fish and insects ripple the water. Still ponds mirror crisp silhouettes of huts and buffalo. To the south, the thin band of cirrus clouds turns pink and the mountains become an inky blue-black on a rose canvas. The moon brightens. Fuzzy young buffalo graze in the bushes by the road and a family sit eating in the dimness of a street-side store and home. The thickening dust and smoke at the edge of town overwhelms my lungs.

*

With a full belly, I sit in the soft light of the veranda of our hotel room, thin green cigar in hand, feet propped up on a neat wooden table and diary in my lap. On the walk home from dinner, I explain to Hiro the meaning of contentment. I say it is what you feel when you've had a big day of activity, and have seen many interesting things, then, tired, you eat a large and delicious meal, and you feel an easy sense of calmness, relaxation and satisfaction; this is contentment.

25

Nyaungshwe, Inle Lake

The timber slat platform with a tin roof on rough-cut poles stands on the side of a steep hill in the forest. Its open sides face slopes covered in a dense green tangle of trees, vines and immense stands of bamboo. A sun-beaten banana tree's leaves hang limp over one corner. The midday chants from Mainthauk Forest Monastery fall over us. The criss-crossed weave of bamboo mats cover the floor where Hiro lies flat on his back, one hand on his chin and the other across his chest. Taxi and scooter drivers chat in the corner and their children wave brooms around. A warm and inconsistent wind comes off the mountain.

Below the monastery, a small creek flows along the valley. Three boys collect water in a plastic bag. A woman in a purple longyi washes herself, head under a cool stream flowing through a half-cut piece of bamboo over a small weir. The bamboo grows tall and thick as a man's thigh. Its yellow-brown leaves lie shiny and smooth on the ground like beached boats after a storm.

Hanging from the roof of the platform is a grotesque fresco of hairy devils torturing a man and boiling young people in a cauldron. I am left to imagine the meaning of the accompanying Burmese script. Against the railings stand two tin people in intricate robes and pagoda-like headdresses. They point at each other with ambivalence. As a baby giggles and screams, the chanting grows stronger and the wind sweeps through the forest with a soft hiss. Someone tinkles a small bell and many young voices rise and begin to chat and laugh.

In the driveway, the car behind a small pickup is covered in the monk's saffron. Leaves fly onto the roof with soft tinging noises. The green hillside heaves and shakes in constant motion; each tree's moving canopy an individual and a part of the forest. Only in the very upper reaches is bare land, which with distance appears motionless. The sky joins it, no clouds to vary its hue, only the sun's slow movement changing its brightness. Spiders crack the sky's perfect palate with their thin grey webs stretching from the poles to the roof.

*

Men and women sit beside the road they build up the steep slopes to the monastery. The road splits into the two-tone grey of today's dark wet line and yesterday's light dry one, the two twining and snaking their way to the lake which shines brilliant silver in the sun. The people crowd around me and comment on my work as I comment on theirs. The road is smooth, with a thick layer of concrete over big orange rocks hewn from the cliffs at the roadside. The wind still blows warm but with strength here to cool down from the work. The slopes even out as the valley widens into plantings of sugarcane and huts. The thick green of rich lakeside crops meets the shore and over the lake's haze the mountains are smoky blue. The men are in great humour. A few smoke idly, crouching and watching. Between laughter they talk in gentle voices. Their scooters make a line up the road. Piles of gravel line the unsurfaced half of the road and a cement mixer and shovel are the only tools apart from their hands. Trees shade the road until it curves out of site.

*

Three groups of tourists come together on three benches to bask in the gentle warmth of the late afternoon sun and witness its brilliant departure from the day's seamless sky. The benches surround a table of the same dark red as the wine from the vines which grow in neat green curves past a small garden below our ledge. The lake is too far south to reflect the sun which instead shines in a thin strip from the narrow channel which connects it to the town. Spot fires from burning sugar cane chaff throw up thick white smoke which a steady southerly wind drives north in long straight lines. The heads of growing sugar cane become white gold with the sun. A pink haze grows in the smoky north with the sun not yet over the mountains. The happy buzz of many tongues rises over the rustling of a shady tree outside the winery's restaurant.

Glasses mount on the table in appreciation of the vines. A couple of middle-age sit next to each other on a bench. The woman tucks her legs up to her chest. They laugh and adjust and readjust and look into each other's eyes. As the sun touches the mountains, people stand and search for the day's great shot. And then the mountains eat the sun, the page dimming as they swallow. An orange haze grows over the southern hills before those of the far north make crisp blue silhouettes on pale washed yellow. The red earth between the vines colours Inle with the same palate as Bagan. The sun leaves a soft orange halo where it fell. It grows cool and a pair of travellers bid farewell. The sugar cane heads shine no more and blend back into the valley floor between clumps of trees. The indistinct town of odd pagodas and houses sits quiet under its dusky shroud.

26

Nyaungshwe to Yangon

Pagoda on pagoda crowd the Inn Dein temple, their slender smooth spires innumerable. They ring the temple in earthly shades, rich terracotta and red brick and faded grey. Close to the centre they are bright and gold and clean and grey with the fresh mortar of repairs. The temple has a tin roof coloured in the varied reds of its sun-worn tint and patches of rust. An eight-levelled tower houses the central Buddha. Its roof is gilded, and fine metalwork hangs from the eaves.

In the background is a rocky outcrop, its steep grey jumble crowned with a handful of gold spires. On the plain, the long, straight lines of bunds between rice paddies lead to dotted farmhouses. The lake and hills disappear in the haze. Bells tinkle from the hilltop pagoda overlooking Inn Dein, the wind swishes through the leaves and a hammer strikes nails one after the other in the village. A pale saffron flag wraps itself around a bamboo pole tied to the trunk of an almond tree.

Tourists holding sandals and cameras wander between the maze of structures. The tin leaves which hang from each pagoda's many small bells move and glitter in the wind. In a cloudless sky, the sun bakes the brick pagodas, which keep their Buddhas cool within. Faint silhouettes inside older pagodas mark the absence of their vanished statuesque inhabitants. They are the shape of centuries of smoky offerings cast over stone Buddhas. Green creepers and thick spiderwebs clothe the rubble. Pagodas yet more ancient become giant flowerpots as thick tree roots crack the bricks and then hold them together anew. The two thousand foot walkway covered in rusted tin snakes west and away through leafy trees.

*

Three young women sit on a bamboo mat with their legs pushed straight against wooden blocks. Looms stretch tight to a rail from belts around their waists. They have upright backs and long necks encased in gold hoops. They wear make-up with pale faces and pink lips and bright scarves in their hair. Their frocks are short on their arms and longyis reach their ankles. They sit by an opening to the balcony which overlooks the river. It roars with the long narrow wooden craft. On the opposite bank is a white temple with a gold-roofed turret at its entrance.

The weavers work with quick neat actions, chatting as they organise their three layers of thread with wooden combs. Their arms and hands dance in fluid movement. One makes a gap in the layers of thread by twisting a comb, throws the reel through and catches it in her other hand. A spindle in front of them turns steadily as an old lady with a very long, thin neck and bands on her calves and ankles winds thread into a ball. They wear wide silver bands and watches on their wrists. From their complex patterns, beautiful scarves emerge, growing out and away from them, before being wound back into the wooden spindles in their laps. They are of the Kayan tribe, shunted from Thailand to Myanmar and bringing their craft with them.

*

Hiro runs out of time to finish showing me a magic trick as we wait for a pickup from the hotel to the bus depot. His sense of humour and tales of a fascinating journey, a cultural cross-section of the world, give the days a great feeling. He is not concerned with the history of a place until tasting it, his travelling experience one of the here and now. A dim restaurant near the bus stop has a few locals inside. We enjoy a quick meal before boarding the overnighter to head south to Yangon.

27

Yangon

Hiro and I leave an internet café to see a Hindu procession. Barefoot men trail bright circles of fabric on wires from their waists. They stamp their feet and jangle like tambourines. Behind them is a wagon drawn by six white Brahman cattle in bright cloths, foaming at the mouth and keen to go on as the crowd presses in and traffic squeezes past with horns honking.

*

A thin man with circular gold-rimmed glasses and a sparse moustache sits cross-legged on the platform of Yangon Central Station. He is cutting individual grapes off their vine. His thick black hair falls to the top of one eyebrow, his skin is a shining brown against his starched singlet and a brown cloth bag hangs around his neck. The bag rests on the blue and white patterned longyi drawn tight between his crossed legs. In front of him are wide shallow palm trays of fruit sitting on blue milk crates and a silver bowl on an analogue scale. His black bomber jacket hangs on the signal pole ladder behind him. Customers come and buy small mandarins in plastic bags. He expertly slices a watermelon along the rind then into thin even sections which he pushes with the knife blade and they drop one by one into the bag. He gets up and a toddler eating a piece of watermelon the size of his head takes his place.

A fat policeman in dark green strolls past the train's open shutters with his beret buttoned to his shoulder. Women walk in and out of the carriage with baskets of eggs in hand or trays of sweet and sour plums on their heads. The eye-watering green plastic benches which line the carriage fill with a drift of tourists and locals. We are both parties curious about the other. Two young British men get on with a mountain bike and bags of lunch to join their parents. A man eats an icy pole in a thin plastic bag. On the neighbouring tracks, a train pulls in and men unload huge bamboo baskets full of greens and covered in sacks and octopus straps. The carriage becomes hot and stuffy as produce and people sweat in the still air. With a rattle, the train strains and pulls away from the platform.

*

At Lammadaw Station, a monk sits waiting on a truck tyre. Tin fences and tarpaulins separate the tracks and the slums. A bare-chested Hindu with a silver chain and a bright blue longyi watches the train leave Pyay Road. A woman on the other side of the carriage nods off. At Shan Road, a man sells quail eggs and the woman wakes when her neighbour gets off the train.

Trees and creepers break apart the bluestone walls to Ahlone Road. Hiro falls asleep as a yawning man opens a copy of *Democracy Today* when jungle breaks into Yangon at Panhlaing Road. We rise from a cutting to the clatter of the train changing tracks and the hammering of smithies at the tin factories of Buddhist iconography. A man scurries on at Kemmendine with a yoke of green bananas. A family sit on a white sheet inside the concrete wall, a boy lies on his back in a hammock, a toddler wears only a dirty shirt and washing dries between the tracks to Hanthawaddy. The exodus continues until the carriage is nearly empty.

New razor wire shines over bamboo by Hletaw. The crowded platform empties and the train fills again. A tourist looks at his camera screen and frowns. Fields of greens grow in murky brown water and cars nose onto the crossing before Kamayut. A painting of Buddha hangs from a tree surrounded by old car tyres. Timber stiles cross the new concrete wall. A canal runs black under the tracks to Thirimyaing. A wooden house with chicken wire windows comes right to the tracks and graffiti grows amongst thick undergrowth in Okkyin. A woman chops up pork by a boiling pot. The smell of betel grows as slowly as a woman chews it with one leg up on the seat. Neat crops show over the wall.

Sandals and bananas on poles welcome us to Thamaing. Concrete posts lie next to empty holes. Colourful beach umbrellas shade the platform of Thamaingmyothit next to the construction site of brick high-rise apartments. A man holding his steel lunch tin coughs on the platform. Palm logs demarcate an open rubbish pile. Gourds grow on trellises. A man lifts the boom gate at Gyogon and traffic floods over the road behind the train.

A man's legs shake underneath his load of a huge bale of plastic. Two black dogs sleep outside two toilet doors. Coils of razor wire crown the wall. Beyond it stand abandoned sheds and a watch tower, before the wall shrinks then vanishes to brown fields and dirt. Soon a fence pops up, then the wall solidifies and train tracks slide underneath a solid steel gate. An old train, paint flaking and bubbled red, rests inside. A soldier leans on his forearm in a wooden watch tower. We are at Insein. Washing hangs between a pole and an upended train axle. Men strain to bend thick steel reinforcing bars as we go under a bridge. The wall says 'happy new year' in thick block lettering. An old Mazda track car collects dust in a shed. Fishing nets dissect a dam.

An orange dirt football pitch at Ywanna has bright white goals. A man washes as a mother inspects her child's hair. A driver's feet poke out from the window of a truck. A water tower peeps over fences thick with creepers at Hpawkan.

Beautiful pink flowers border the line. Giant yellow gantries stand over piles of scrap metal. Men with a near-empty whiskey bottle chat next to the tracks. The wall is immense now and volleyball nets meet its base at Aungsanmyo. Music plays from a man's phone. Housing flat balconies are clothed but bare of people. A young boy in bare feet and a shirt with a union jack across the shoulders runs away. Tall factories dwarf the fields and huts. Berries spread on mats dry in the sun between the tracks coming into Danyingon.

The smell of piss floats from the crowded platform. Shouts from the end of the carriage then laughter. A man passes a heavy sack through the windows wearing a 'Young Engineers Excursion' T-shirt. Bananas are shifted up and over the produce into the doorway. The pink flowers are dusty.

To the east is open farmland, to the west roads, and smokestacks jump over the thin strip of crops. A woman cuts open fruit for her baby son who looks open-eyed at me for a while until we stop at a station called Golf Course.

The horizon widens to farms on both sides of the tracks. The orange-clothed baby takes tiny bites of the fruit. His name is Wan Wie and his mother wipes his face before he looks at the camera with cautious eyes. He eats the peanuts I give him from the palm of one hand at Kyaikkale. Wan Wie stops eating and sits with his right hand propping him up and his leg on a sack. The train rises up an embankment. A big walnut tree shades crops of watercress. Buffalo graze fields as the train goes east through Mingaladon Bazaar.

Wan Wie throws a nut on the ground. A plane comes in to land. Children wave from a hut and farmers wade through ponds. At the edge of a village with no station, the train stops. Flies buzz around as a man propped up in the corner plays a game on his phone. Pigs lie in a small enclosure with its own bamboo bridge over the ditch. Birds dart over the fields as another plane comes in. We roll on. Traffic banks up on a six-lane road and brick buildings hedge the northern way into Mingaladon.

A Hindu lady crosses her arms as the train passes, a *thanaka*-cheeked girl picks her nose and a farmer's hat is stuck on a barbed wire fence. A raised road cracked in the middle runs beside the tracks. Lush green rice paddies appear. Farmers order the crops with long strings tied between bamboo poles. The platform at Waibarge has poles between tree stumps and trees as benches. I give Wan Wie balloons as the family make ready to go, and his mother scolds him. Okkalapa, Wan Wie's house. He waves goodbye standing on the platform.

Loose strings in harvested ponds collect leaves. Huge sacks of plastic bottles mark Paywetseikkon Station. A girl in a T-shirt with 'amore' on it holds a twenty-litre drum of water. A coconut hangs in a basket from a tree. The carriage fills with the smell of dried fish. Rubbish thickens in a single moment from the odd patch to a full carpet. We round the northern limit of the line. Heading south the farms are on the outside still, the east.

A pond at Kyaukyedwin Station is full of watercress and rubbish floating on the green scum. A frowning man approaches the station with flowers over his shoulder. An invisible megaphone blares through the carriage.

A man with a plastic tray on a strap makes betel leaves as we arrive at Tadagale. He taps a man on the shoulder and holds up two fingers. The man nods and he sits down to work with deft fingers, adding powder to the nut which sits in a paste-covered leaf. He stuffs them in a plastic wrapper and leaves with no money.

Roads close in on the farmland, the concrete wall returns and red steel beams rise over it. The cut-off roof of a pickup truck makes a shelter next to the tracks. A man with a tattooed back washes by Yegu Station.

Boys walk along the top of a huge steel pipe. White egrets stand in a black pond. A farmer waters two furrows of his crop at a time with two long-nosed watering cans strapped to a yoke. The platform at Paryame is shady and cool. A man sleeps with his head out the window. Indian myna birds scavenge the bunds where bamboo stands yellowed by the sun. A building has tarpaulin curtains and Kanbe Station has a fence of cyclone wine. 'Enjoy life' urges a Grand Royal Whiskey T-shirt. Red-dotted Hindus talk in unfamiliar tones. A painted Buddhist temple soars from an unremarkable tin roof. Two workers in orange vests clear out a concrete rubbish bin. Car bumpers sit on a shed's roof and the smell of oil and metal is strong in the air. Razor wire caps the wall as houses creep to within a few yards of the track at Bauktaw.

A sleeping pup has the long concrete bench all for itself. A farmer prunes vines. Cauliflower crops and washing monks approach the door of a clinic on the way into Tamwe. An old, dust-grimed man smoking a green cigar sits cross-legged on the long bench, writing on a wad of paper on his knee. With my diary resting on my knee as I sit cross-legged on the carriage's bench, I scratch the old man onto the page as the train jerks onwards without him.

Boys climb over the tall new wall into secrecy. At Myittarnyunt a man with a long wet mohawk puts greens from a pond in a floating bucket and young girls wait for the train. The embankment of an intersecting railway is burnt black. Petrol tankers lounge on the far track and high-rise apartments loom over the platform at Mahlwagon, where grass grows between every crack. Green coconuts cluster around palm centres. The air cools, tall trees and bananas grow among open houses. The train sways violently past three children sitting on the tracks while a freight train clanks and crawls along. A woman walks over a steep wooden stile.

At Pazundaung, thin Hindu girls wear *thanaka*. Young Buddhist nuns sit in a big group around a roof column. Two women and a toddler wave. Sparrows hop on and off the tracks, smoke leaves traces in the air. Downtown streets flash over gaps in the wall. Pot plants line a balcony. A monastery sits in the 'V' of two divergent sets of tracks. Blue gauze covers bamboo scaffolding around a new building topped with a pagoda. An arched window frame rises its whole height of four storeys. The train stops and the sound of crows cawing rises before the train toots and rolls on. A shady garden peeks deep green through an open gate. The train slows, rattles past the fat policeman and the fruit seller, and we complete a circle and come to a halt.

*

In the afternoon, I crawl along like the old train, clanking along familiar rails. A local bus leaves me on a crowded road with a busy market stretching down a side street. After buying some Myanmar cigars and gifts, I find a quiet table and eat fried rice and egg with a small bowl of chilli and lettuce. With a drop of green tea and a finger, I rinse the china cup, flick it into the gutter and pour a fresh cup. When the pot runs out, I ask in flowing Burmese for another. The man at the restaurant smiles.

Hiro and I wander around the People's Garden, a peaceful park of ornamental trees and koi-filled ponds. As the sun sets, we walk outside Shwedagon Pagoda, sitting high on a set of stairs with bats flying from the trees and the spire's gold dimming. Back in the centre of town, we find a restaurant so poky it is a novelty, eating in a five-foot-high second storey with miniature tables and chairs. We feel like giants and the waiter takes a photo of us, heads bent to stand.

It is a hot night, the city abuzz, the traffic busy and the streets full. Yet the roads are easier to cross, food easy to find, the chaos less chaotic. We enjoy our last few hours together, wandering around town, finding the obelisk, circling Sule Pagoda from outside.

I ask Hiro what he would have done if we hadn't met.

'Same thing,' he says, 'walking, walking and seeing.'

He snores on the other bed, face down and fully clothed, exhausted. I savour my final hours, reflecting on the fascination of the place and the people, and as I go to sleep my mind jolts back to the platform at Tamwe and the view of a part of myself out the window. Peace to you, wherever you rest your head tonight, old man.

www.ingramcontent.com/pod-product-compliance
Lightning Source LLC
Chambersburg PA
CBHW030912080526
44589CB00010B/270